Mel Bay Presents

Christmas
ENCYCLOPEDIA
FINGERSTYLE GUITAR EDITION
by Steve Eckels

1 2 3 4 5 6 7 8 9 0

Visit us on the Web at www.melbay.com — E-mail us at email@melbay.com

Contents

(see page 114 for Alphabetical Listing)

Angels from the Realms of Glory

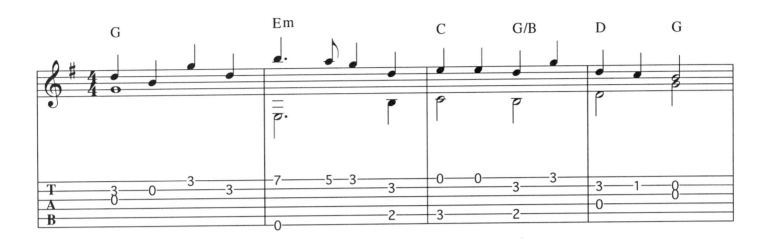

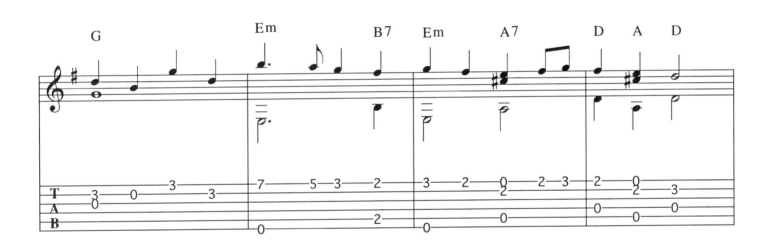

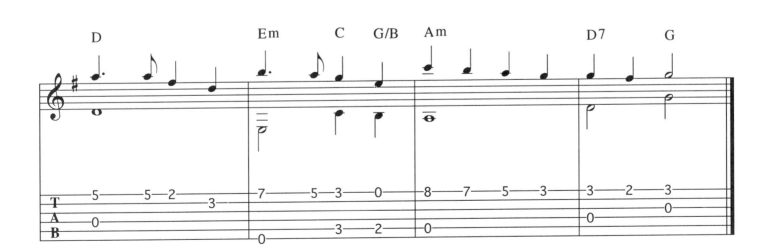

Angels We Have Heard on High

I play this with a
joyful pop/rock feel

Syncopation ad lib

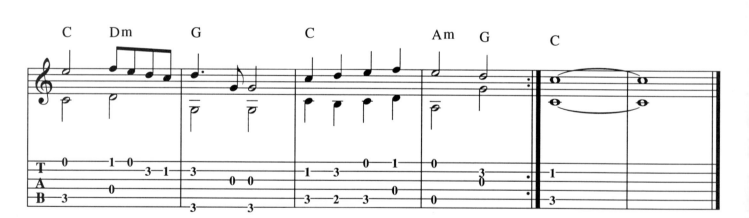

Optional Introduction

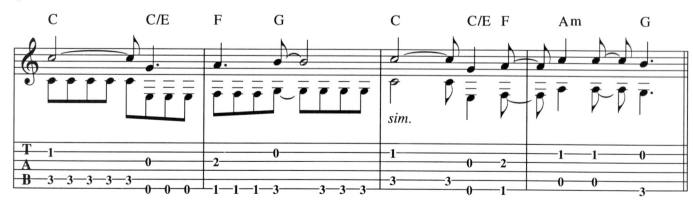

sim.

As Lately We Watched

Ave Maria

Franz Schubert

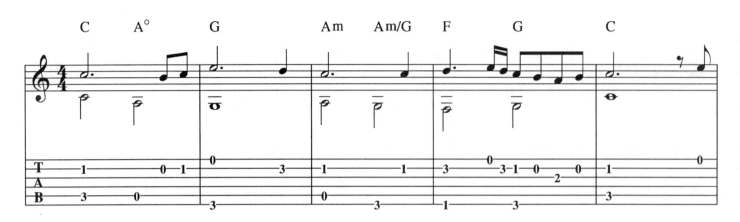

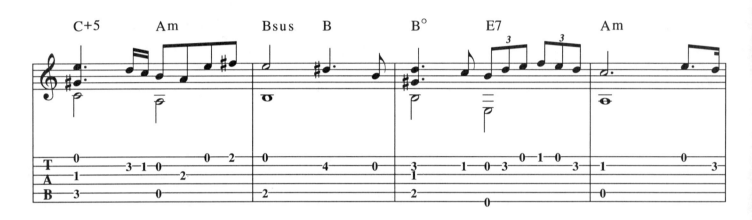

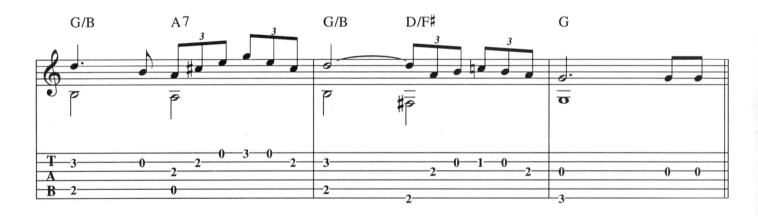

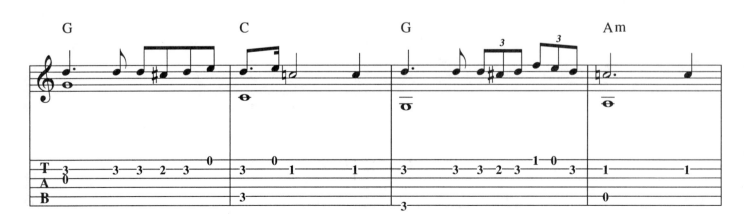

7

Away in a Manger

Key of G

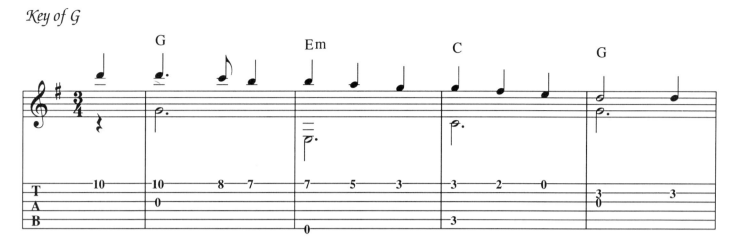

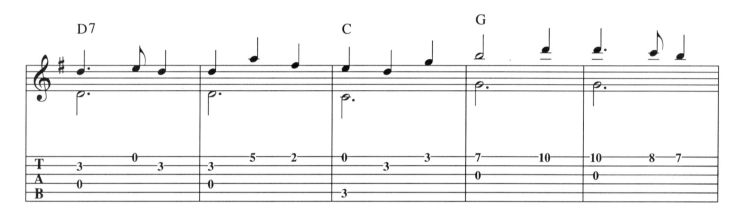

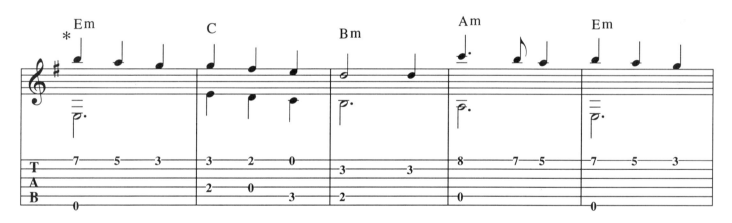

Optional measure

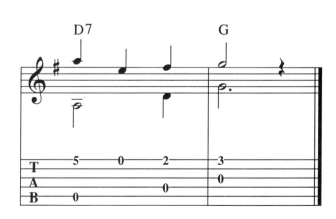
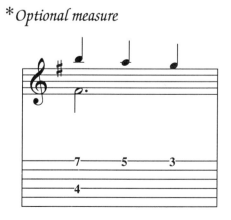

Away in a Manger

English Version

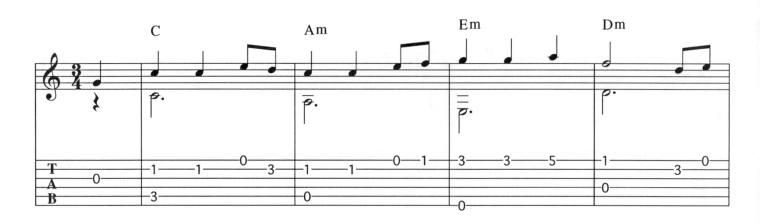

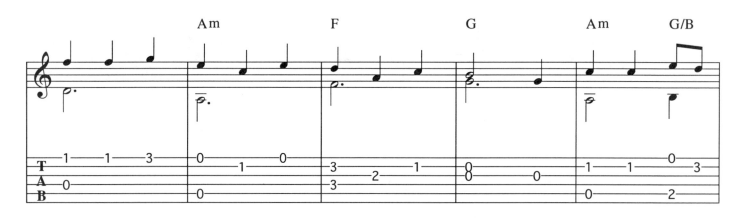

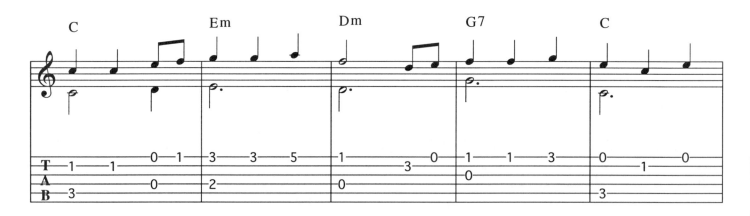

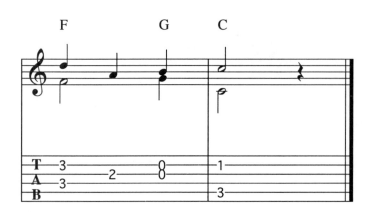

This page has been left blank to avoid awkward page turns.

Bring a Torch, Jeanette Isabelle

Key of G

Bring a Torch, Jeanette Isabelle

Key of C

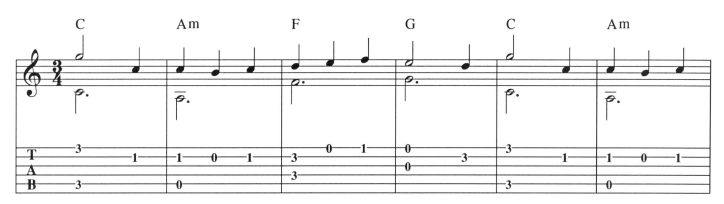

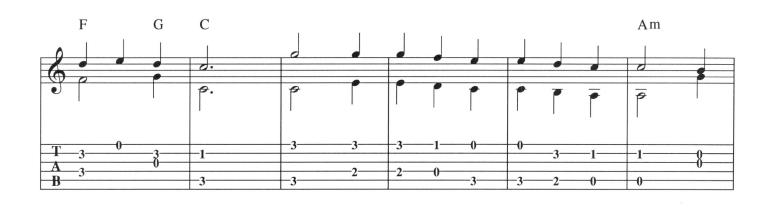

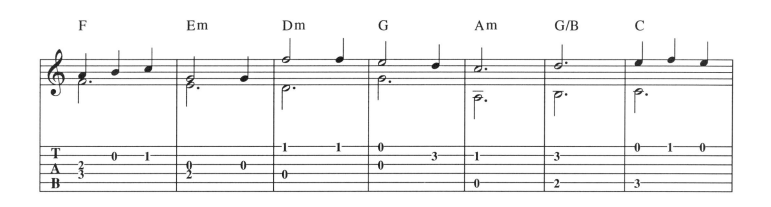

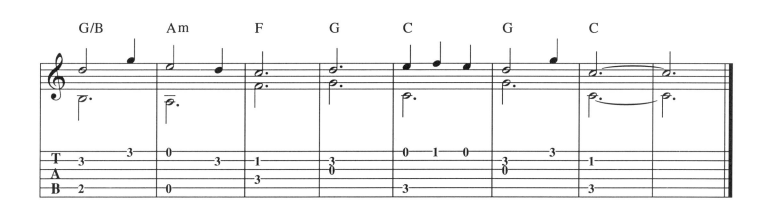

Carol of the Bells

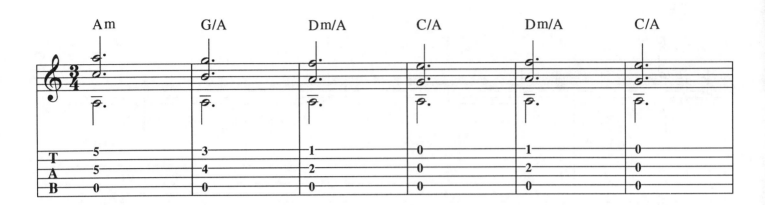

Carol of the Birds

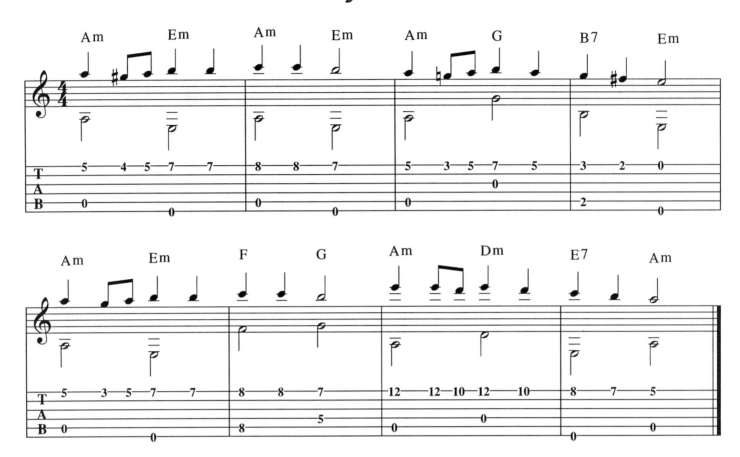

Hush My Babe, Lie Still and Slumber

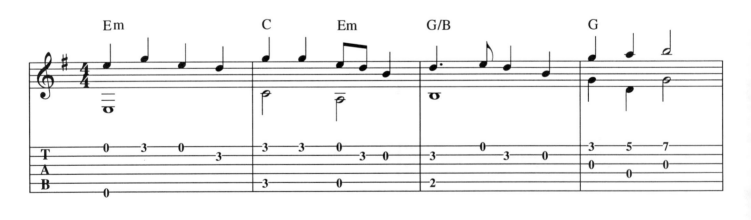

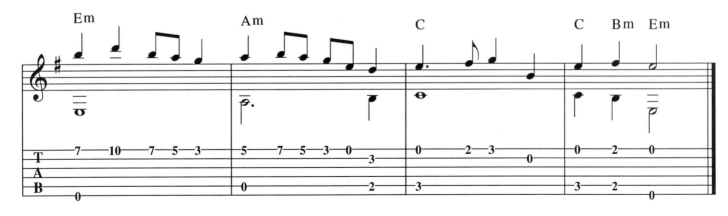

The Christmas Concerto
(Pastorale)

A. Corelli

Baroque Style

add ornaments freely

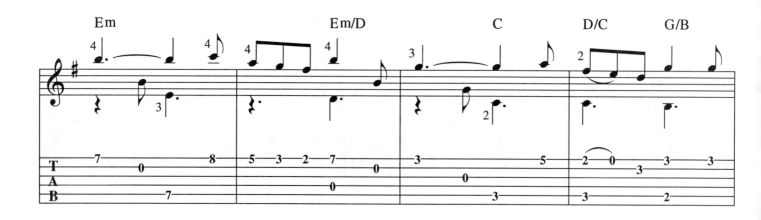

To Coda

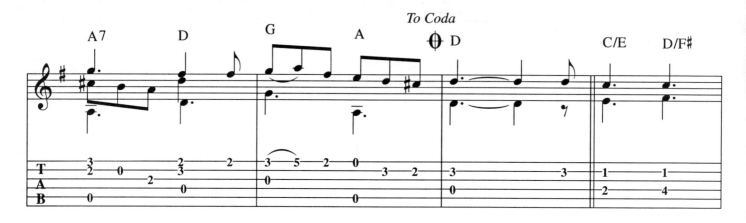

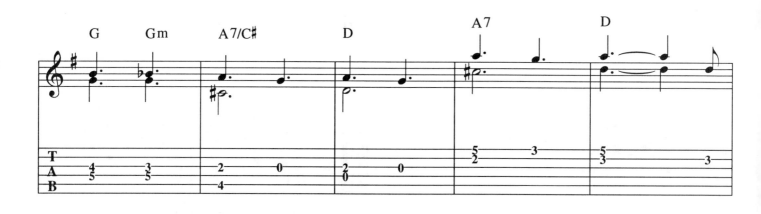

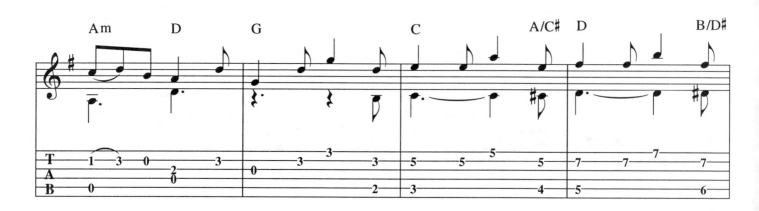

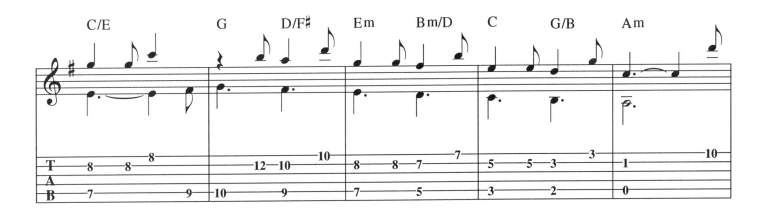

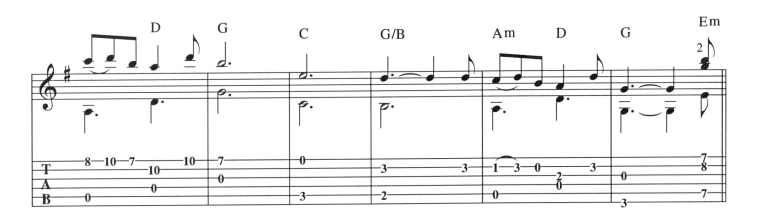

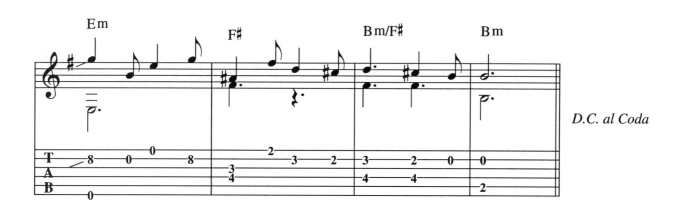

D.C. al Coda

Coda ⊕

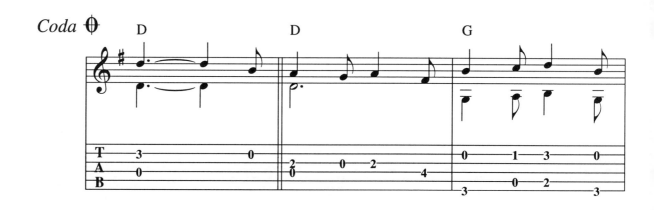

20

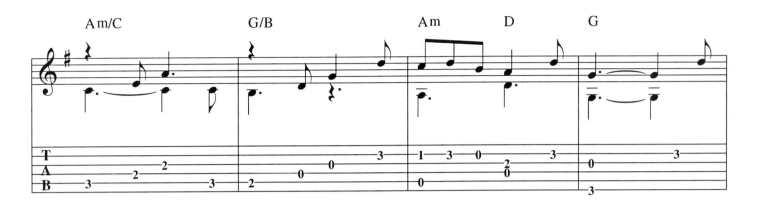

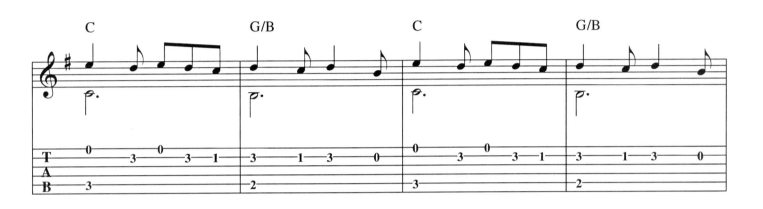

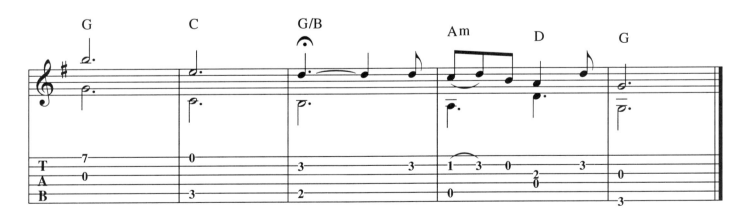

Coventry Carol

Key of A minor

Introduction

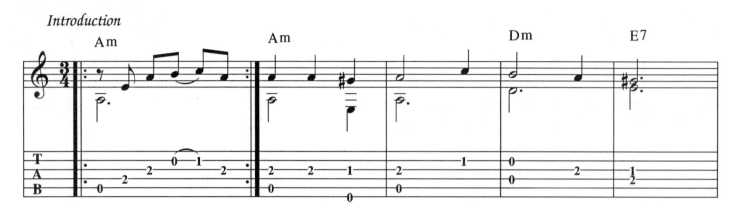

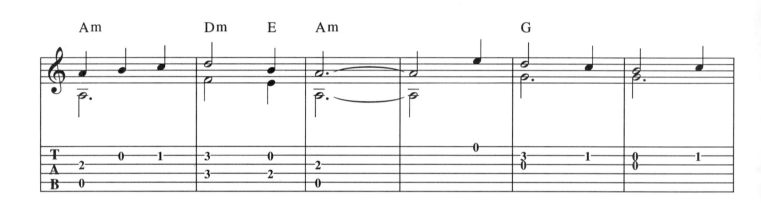

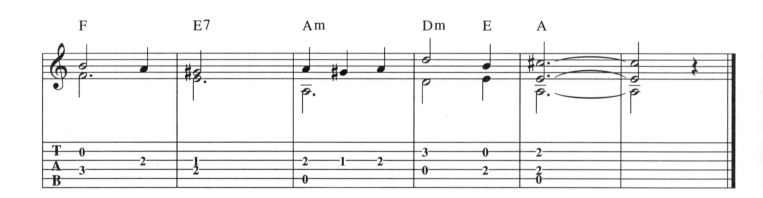

Optional intro or ending

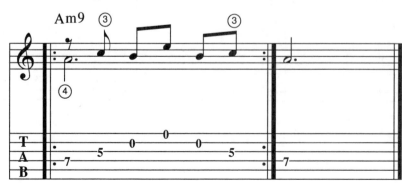

Coventry Carol

Key of D minor

This is one of my personal favorites,
it fits the guitar very well.

Introduction

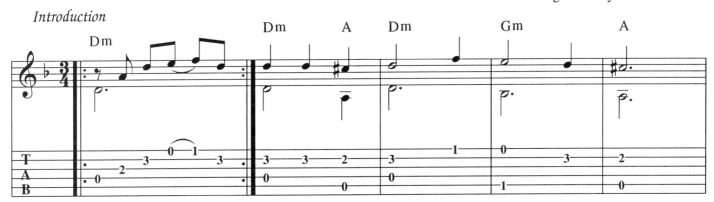

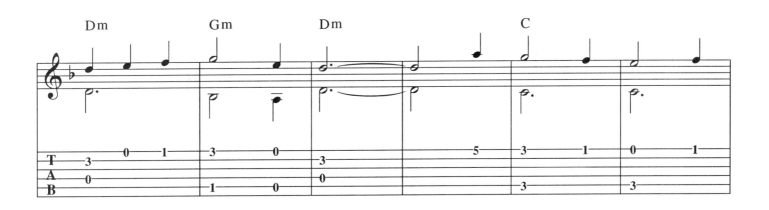

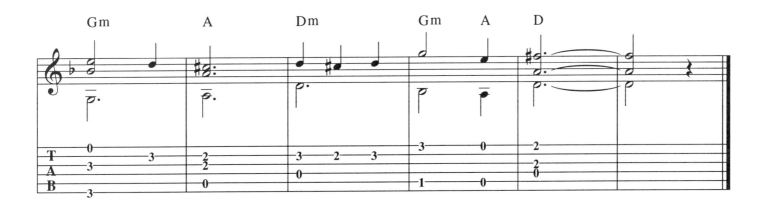

Optional intro or ending

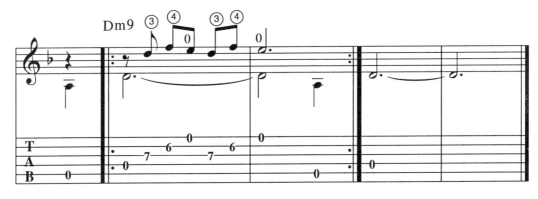

Deck the Halls

Key of C

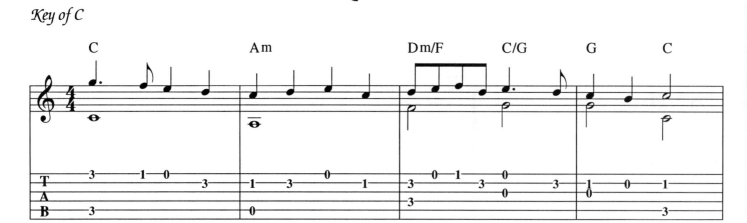

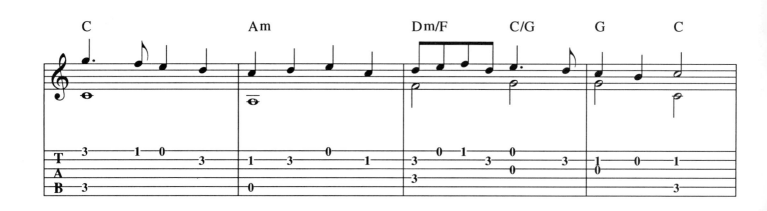

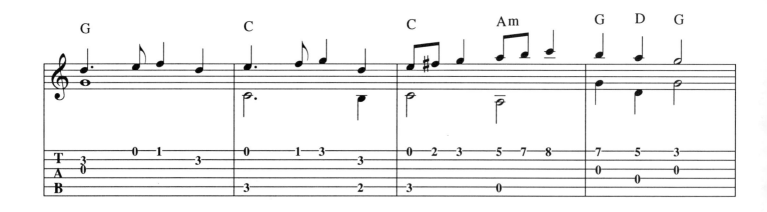

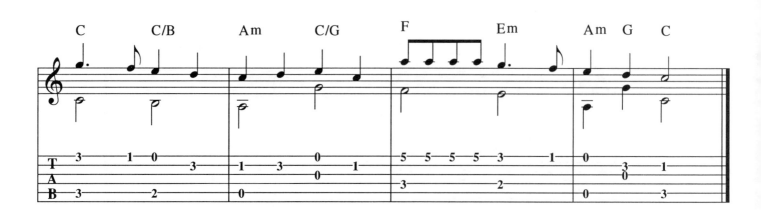

Deck the Halls

Key of D

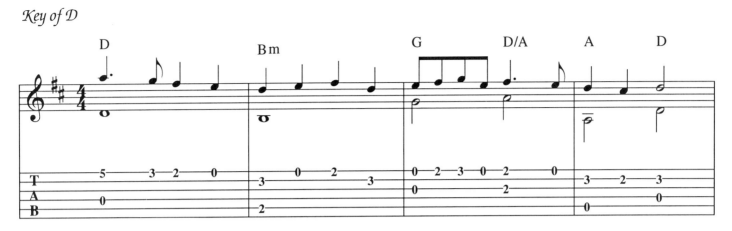

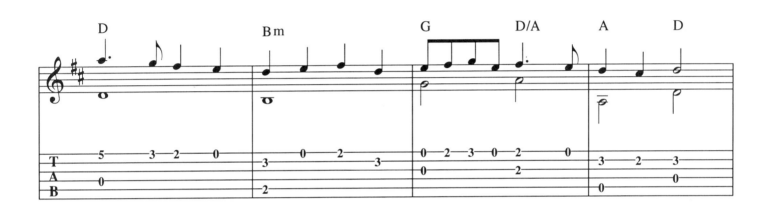

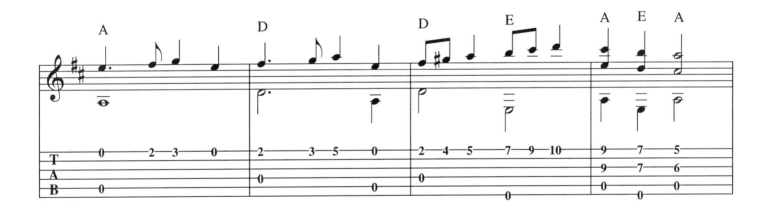

Early Christmas Morn'

13th Century English

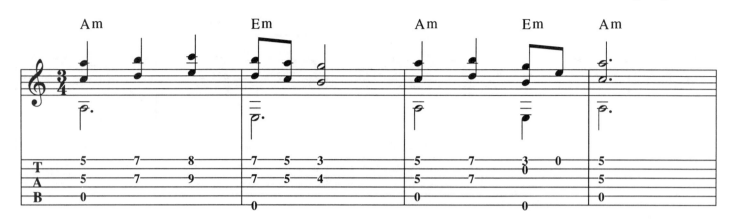

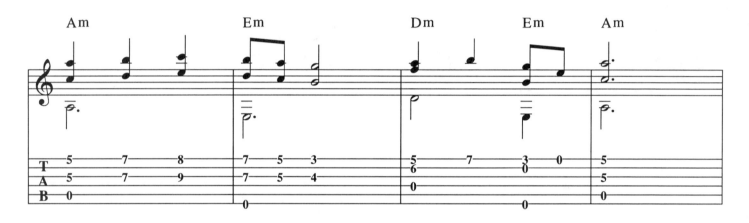

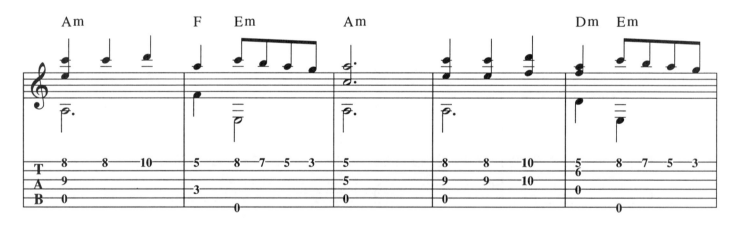

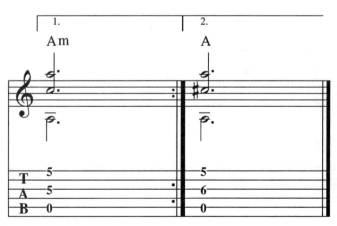

This page has been left blank to avoid awkward page turns.

The First Noel

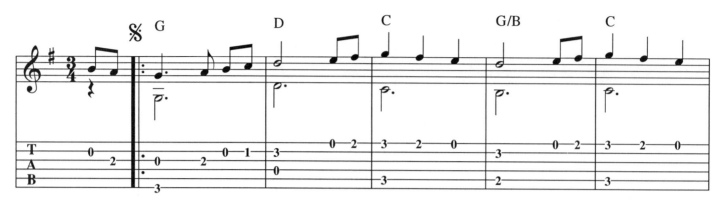

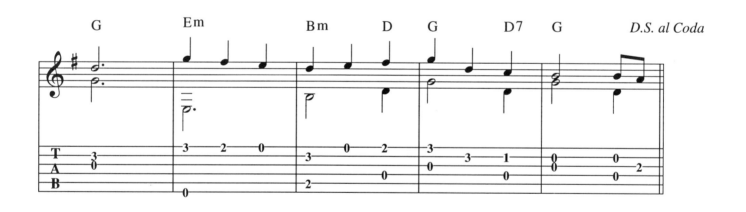

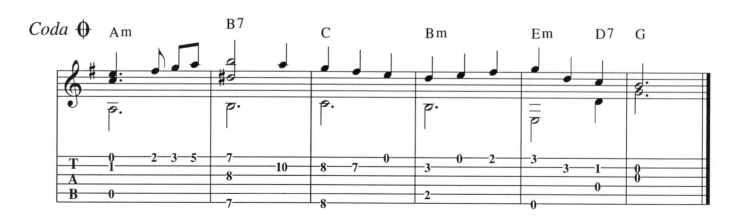

The First Noel

Key of C

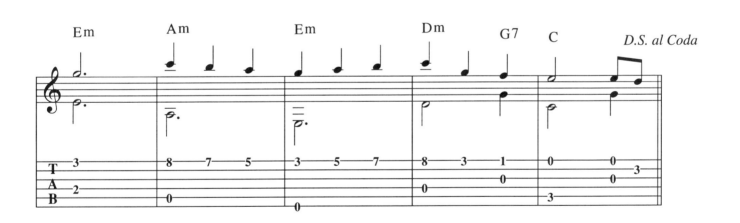

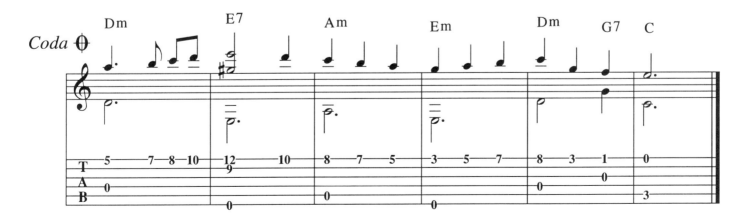

The Friendly Beasts

Key of C

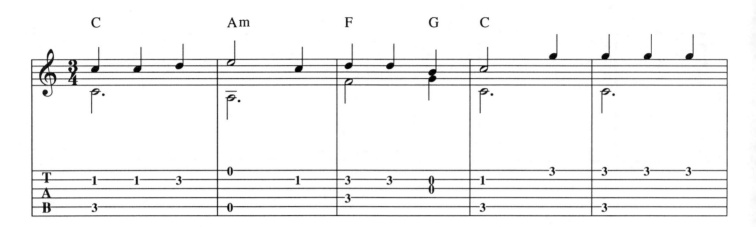

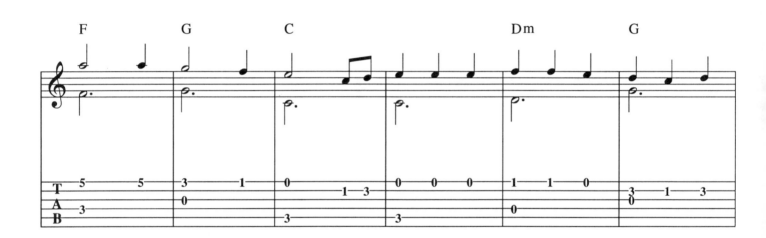

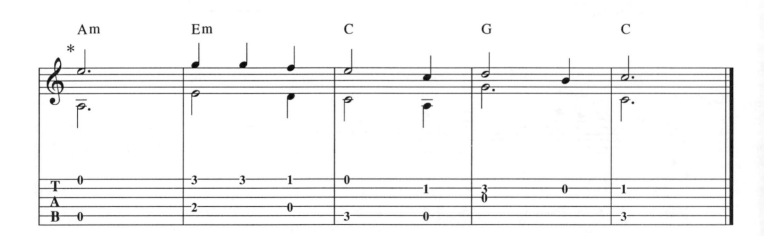

* For contrast, you may sustain this chord for more time.

The Friendly Beasts

Key of D

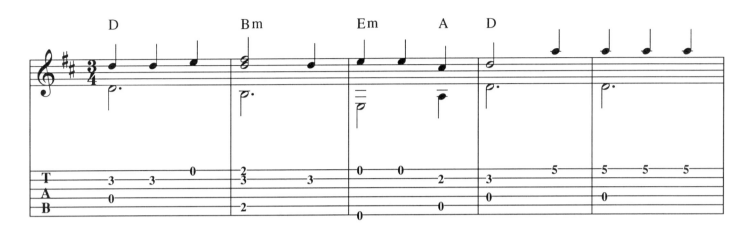

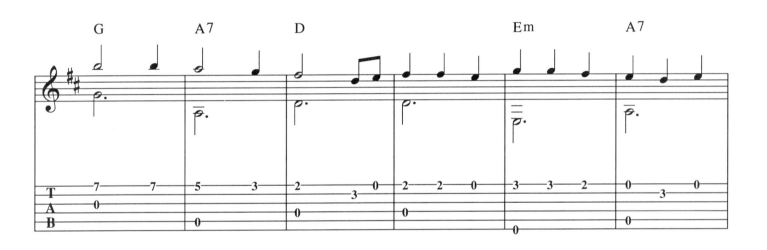

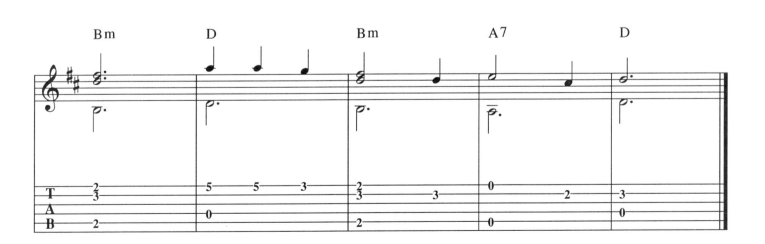

Go Tell it on the Mountain

Key of C

This works well with a
bluegrasss picking style

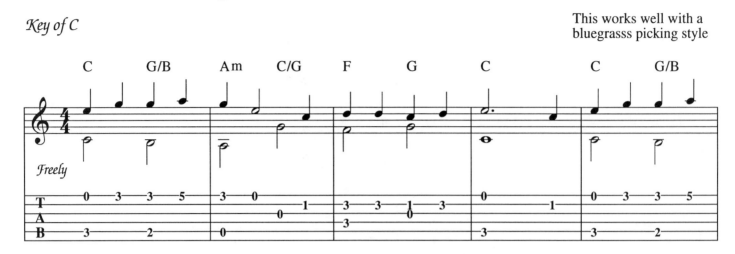

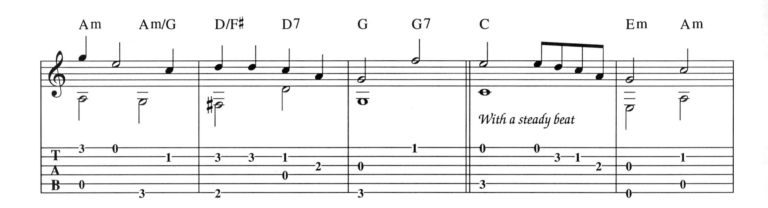

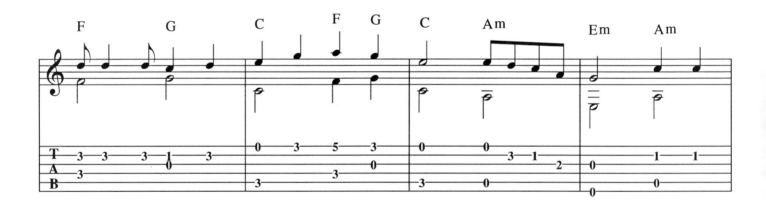

Optional picking pattern

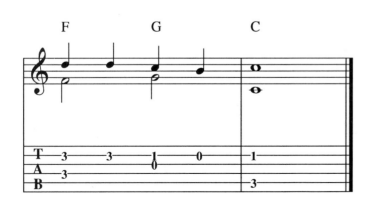

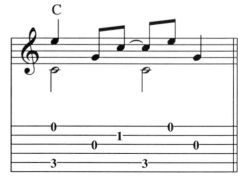

32

Go Tell it on the Mountain

Key of G

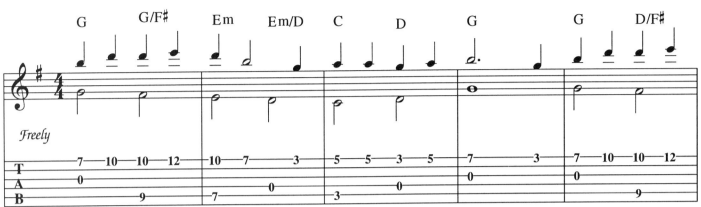

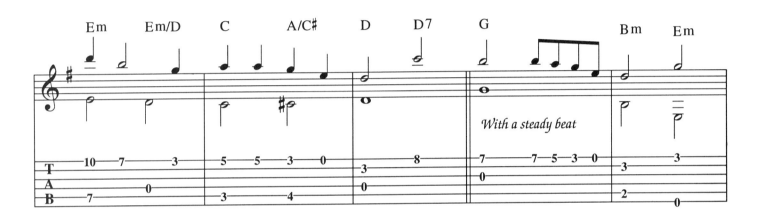

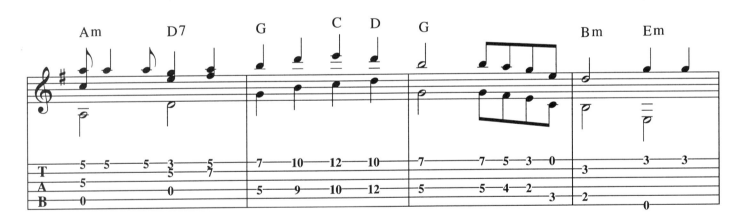

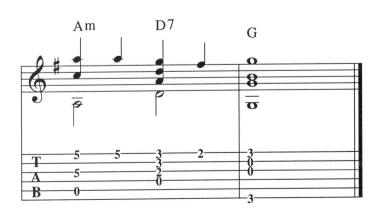

God Rest Ye Merry Gentlemen

Key of A minor

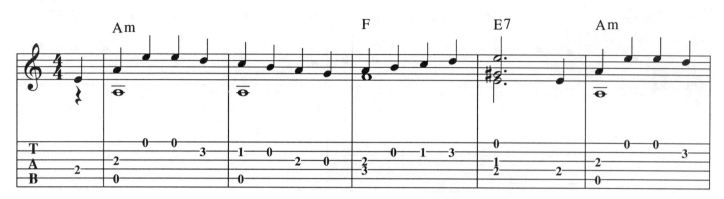

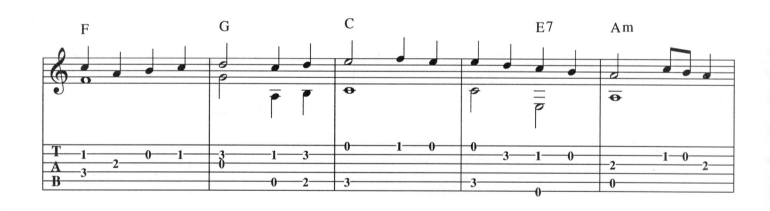

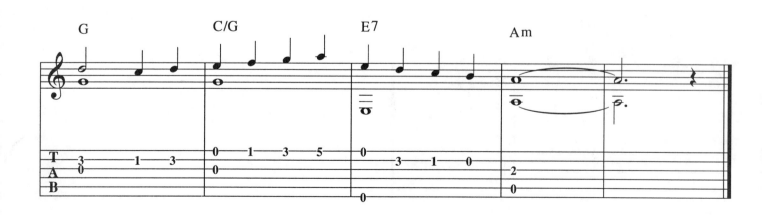

God Rest Ye Merry Gentlemen

Key of E minor

Good Christian Men Rejoice

Key of D

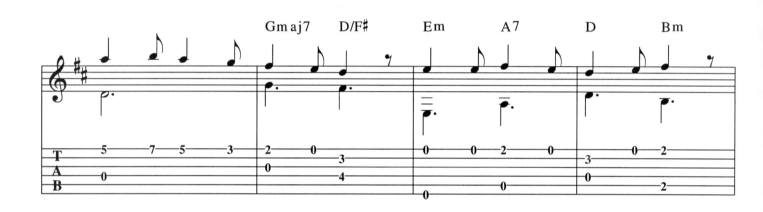

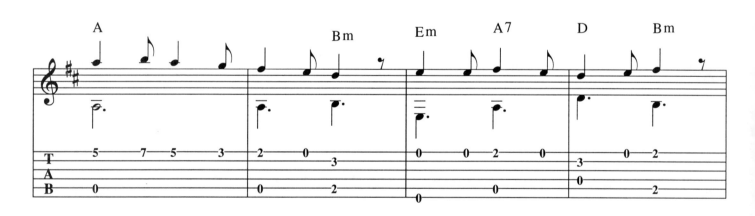

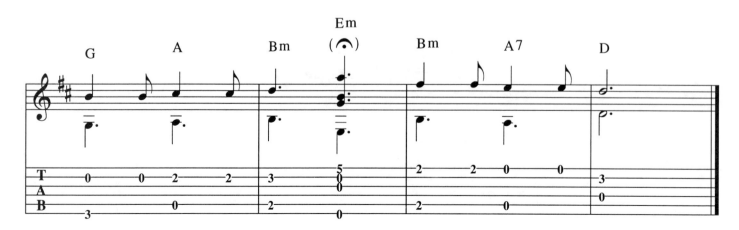

Good Christian Men Rejoice

Key of G

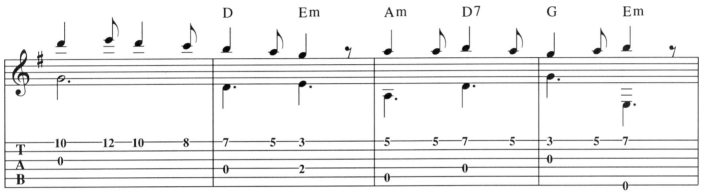

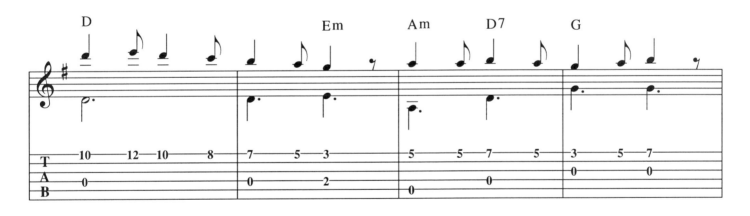

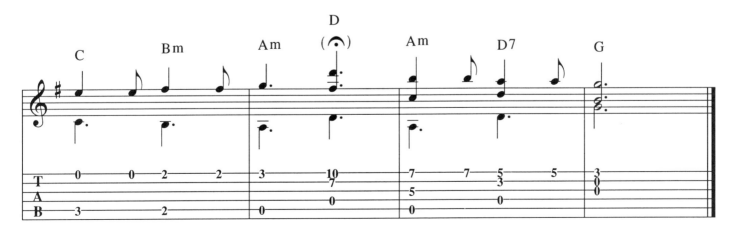

Good King Wenceslas

Key of G

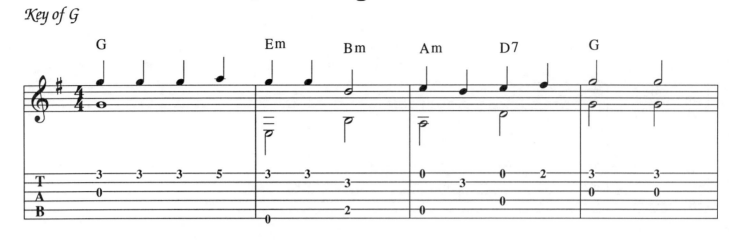

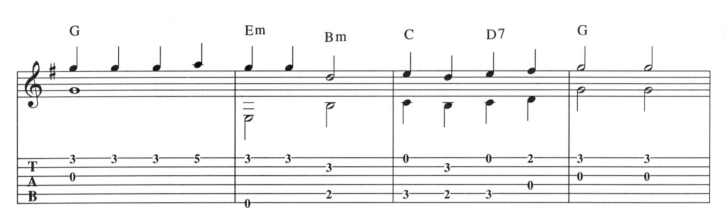

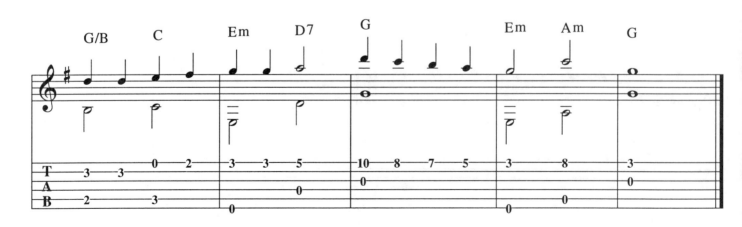

Good King Wenceslas

Key of D

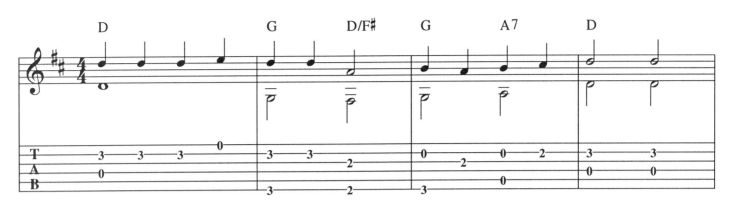

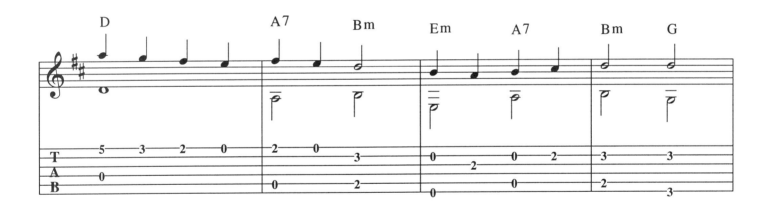

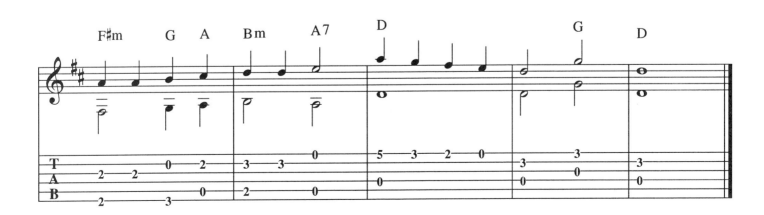

Hark the Herald Angels Sing

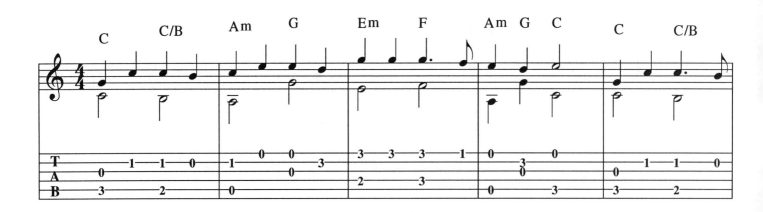

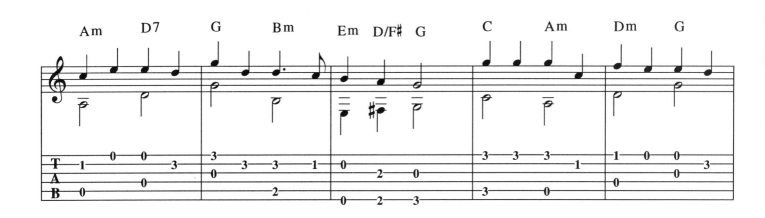

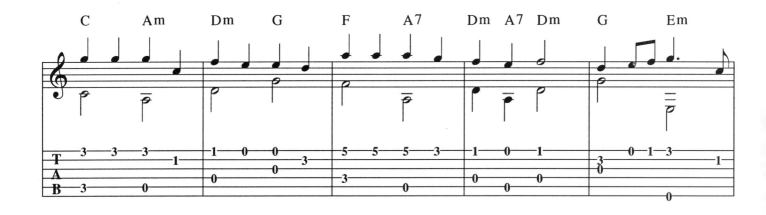

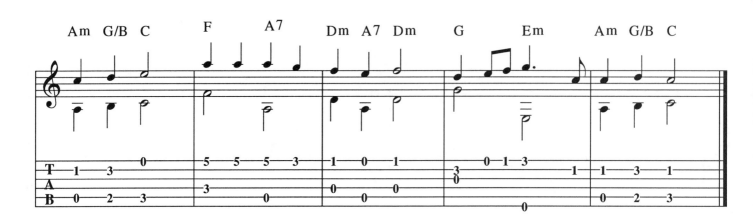

This page has been left blank to avoid awkward page turns.

Here We Come A-Caroling
The Wassail Song

Key of C

Here We Come A-Caroling
The Wassail Song

Key of G

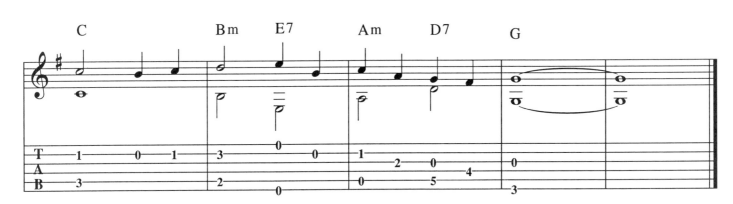

* Pre-plant the 2nd and 3rd fingers on strings 4 and 5.

Hey, Ho, Nobody Home

Key of D minor

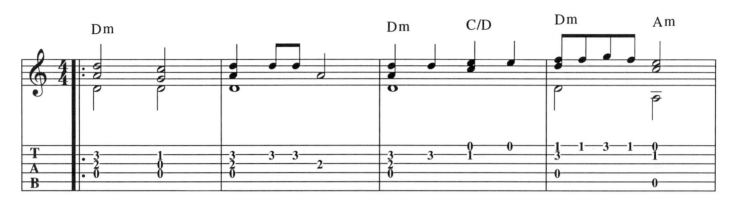

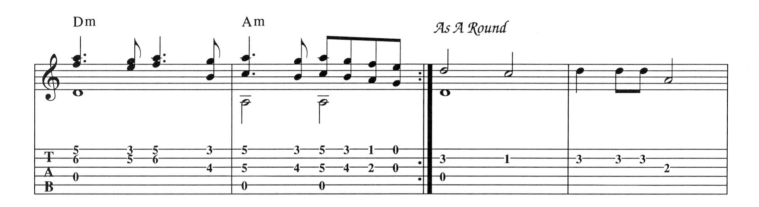

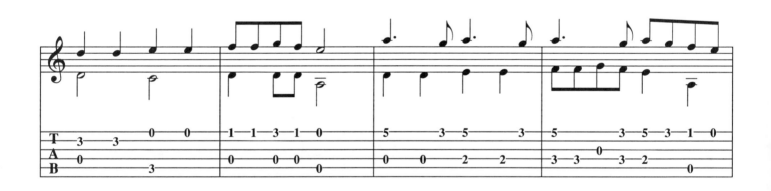

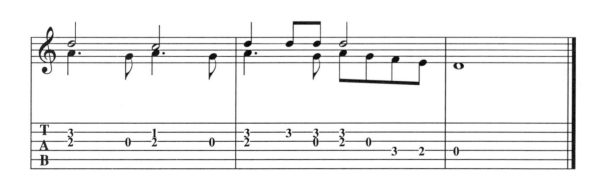

Hey, Ho, Nobody Home

Key of E minor

Introduction

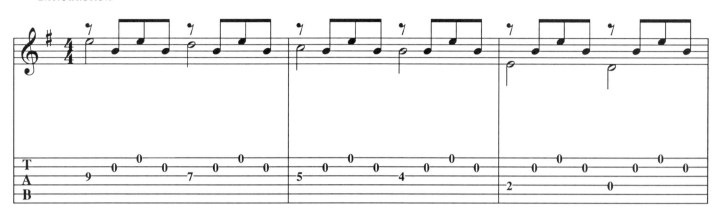

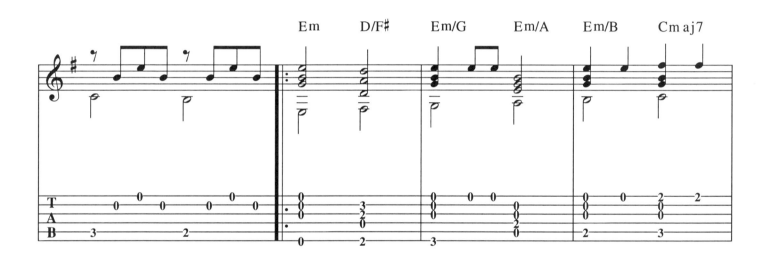

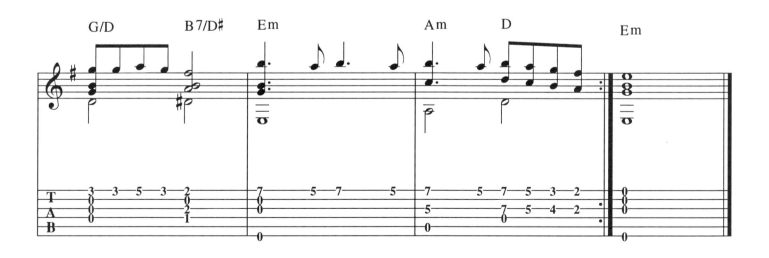

The Holly and the Ivy

Key of G

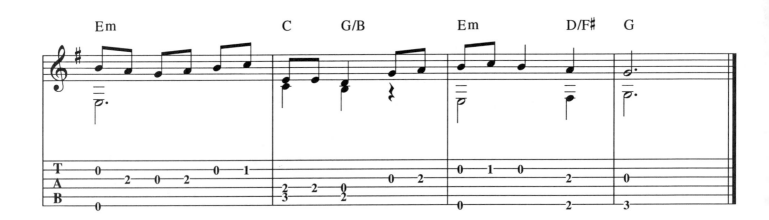

The Holly and the Ivy

Key of C

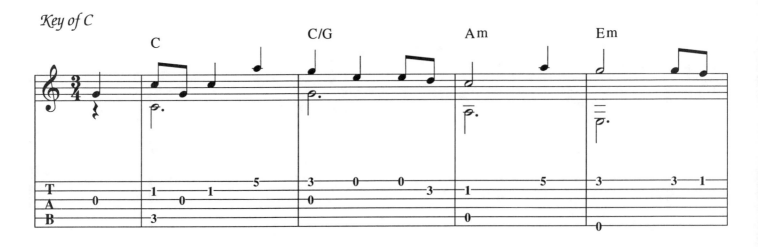

The Holly and the Ivy

Key of D

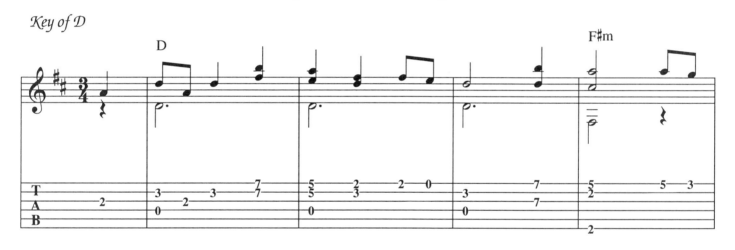

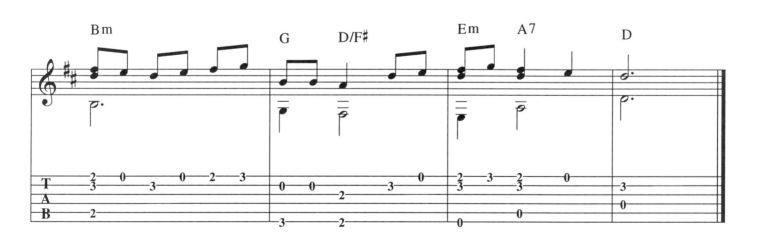

I Saw Three Ships

Key of C

Variation

I Saw Three Ships

Key of D

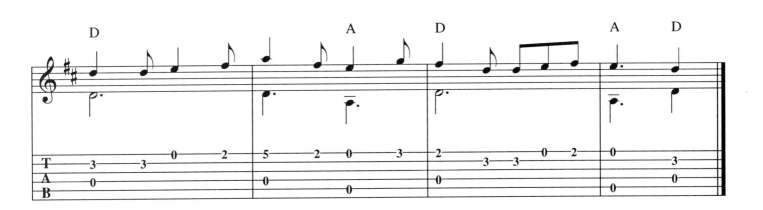

Variation

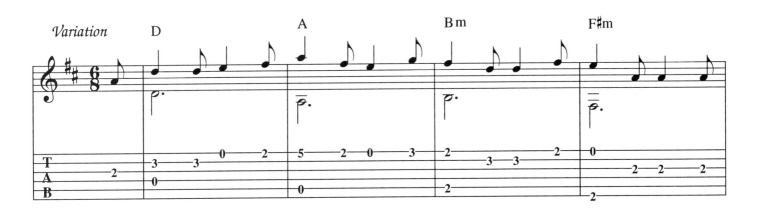

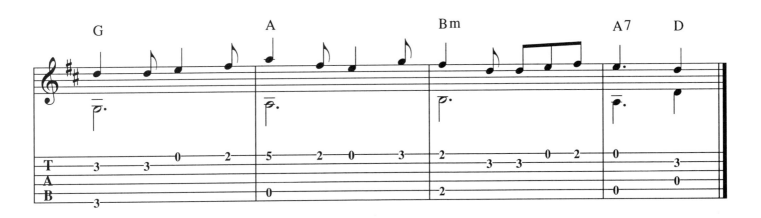

It Came Upon a Midnight Clear

Key of D

It Came Upon a Midnight Clear

Key of G

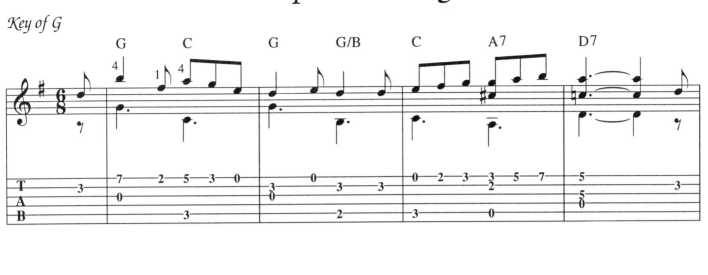

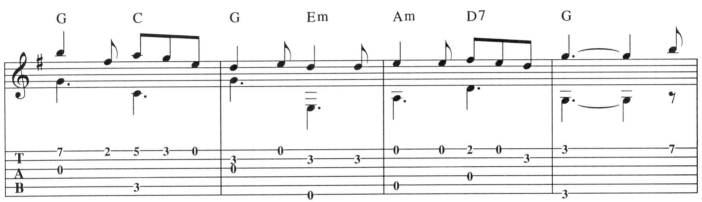

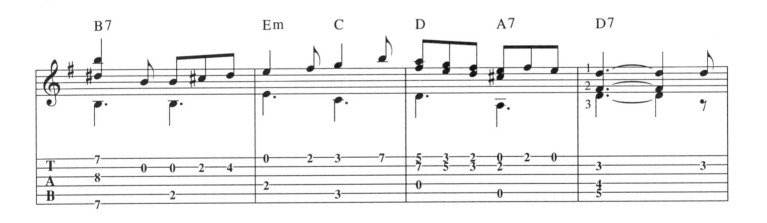

Jesu, Joy of Man's Desiring

Key of G

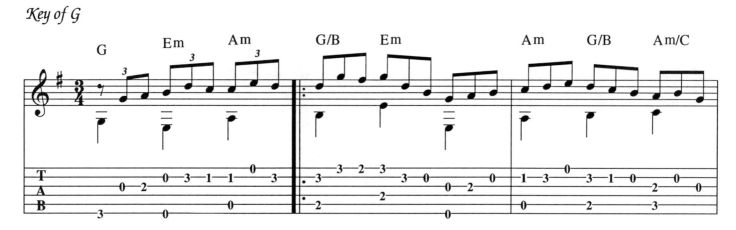

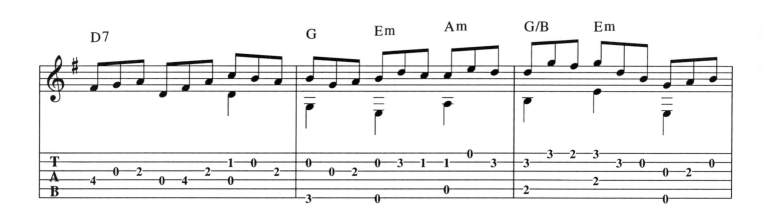

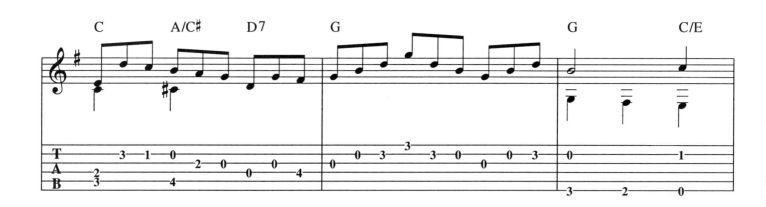

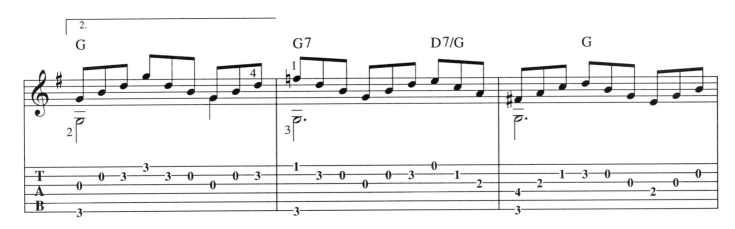

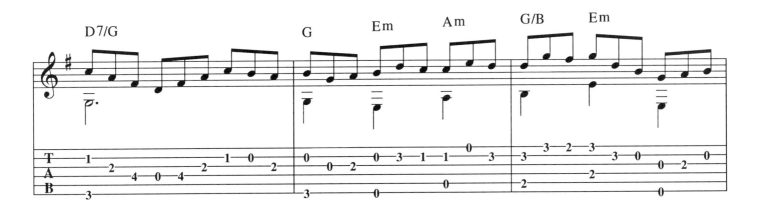

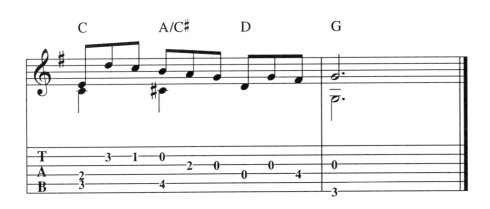

Jesu, Joy of Man's Desiring

Key of C

J. S. Bach
adaptation by Steve Eckels

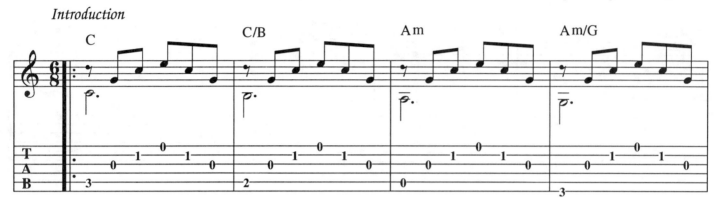

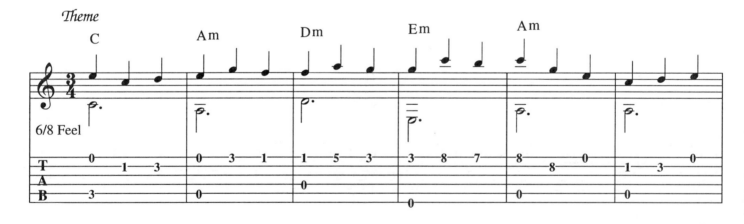

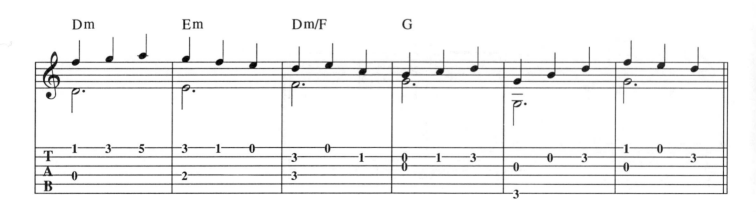

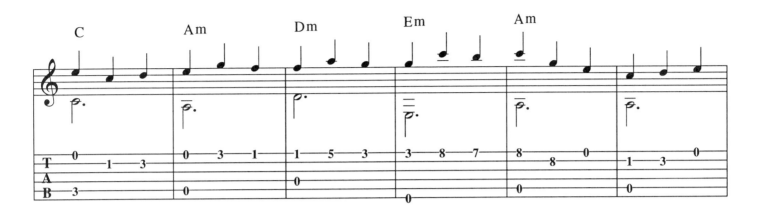

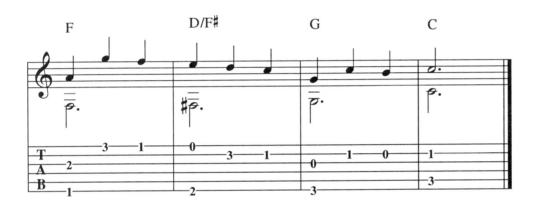

Jingle Bells

This is an excellent study
of triads and Travis picking

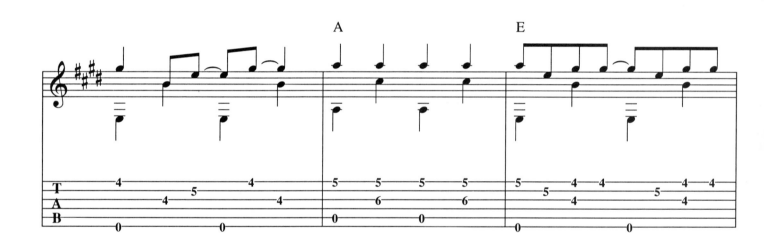

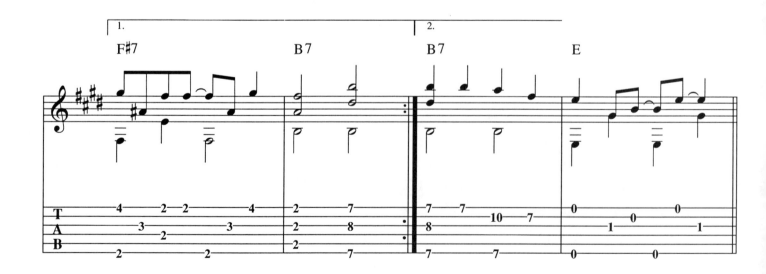

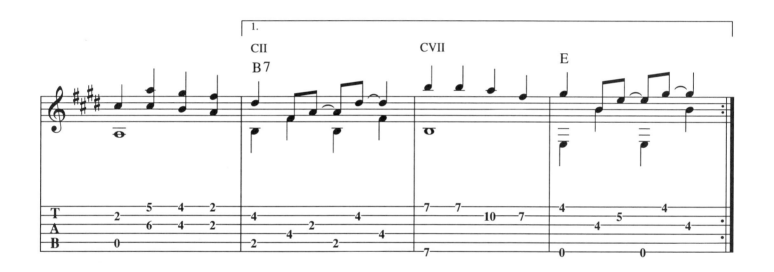

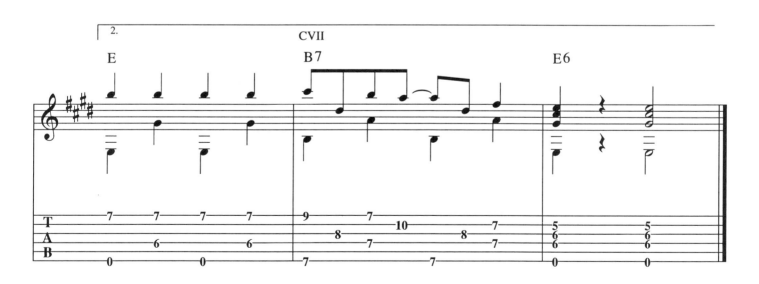

Jingle Bells

I play this with a
bouncy Travis picking feel

58

This page has been left blank to avoid awkward page turns.

Joy to the World

Key of G

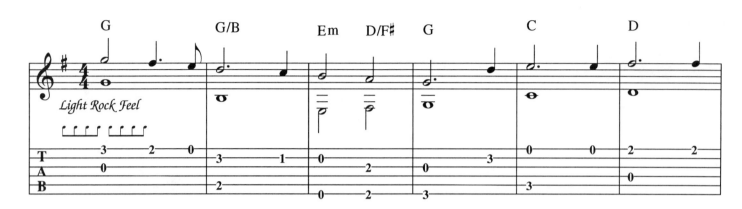

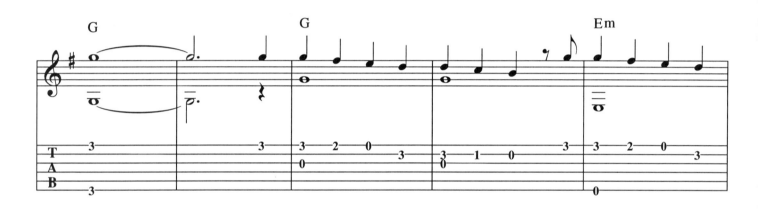

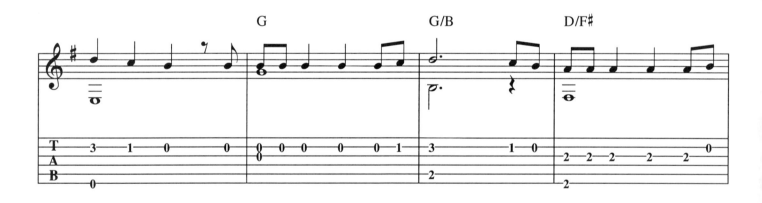

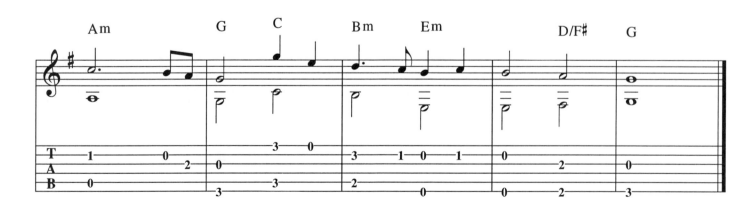

Joy to the World

Key of D

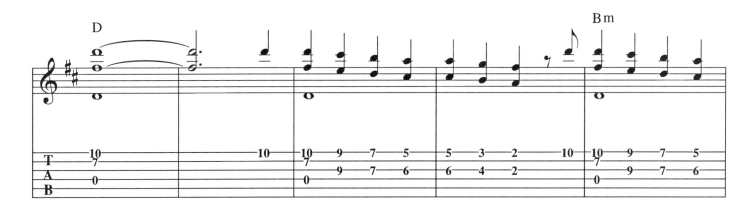

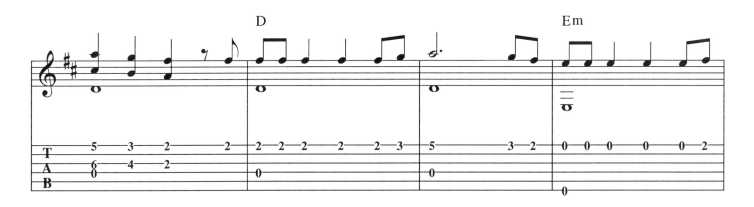

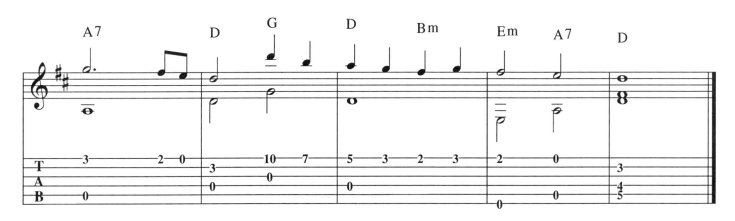

Lo How a Rose E're Blooming

Key of C

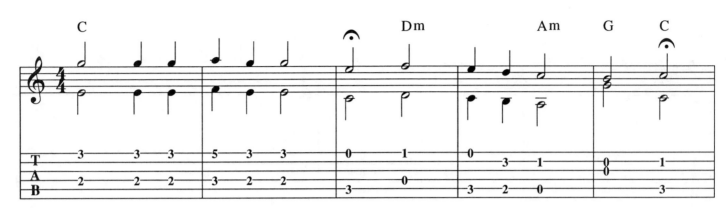

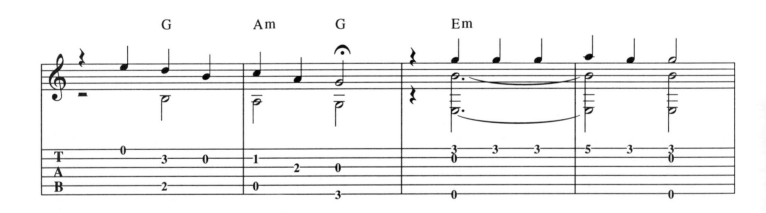

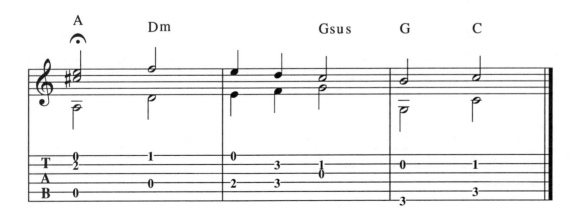

Lo How a Rose E're Blooming

Key of G

Masters in this Hall

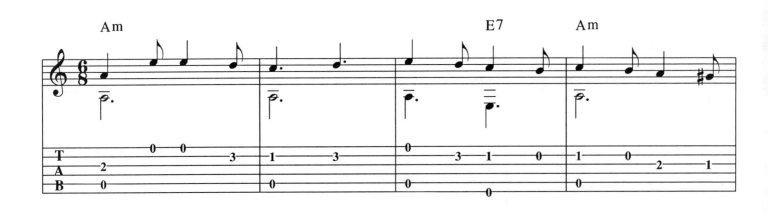

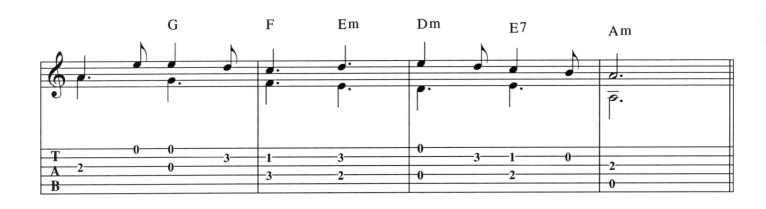

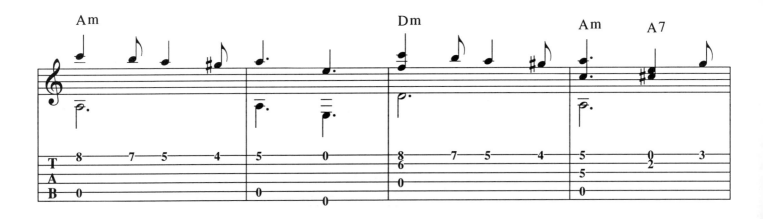

Dance of the Sugar Plum Fairy

from "The Nutcracker"

P. I. Tchaikovsky

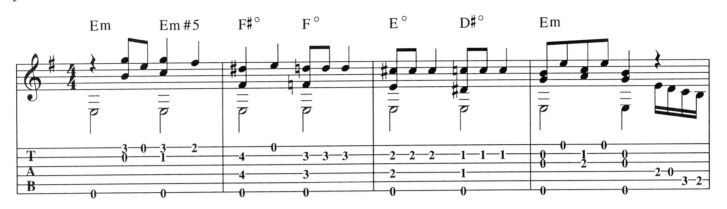

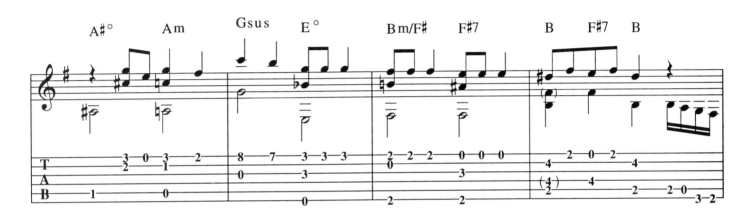

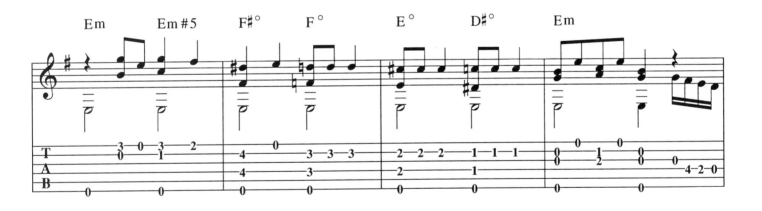

March of the Toy Soldiers

from "The Nutcracker"

P. I. Tchaikovsky

Russian Dance

from "The Nutcracker"

P. I. Tchaikovsky

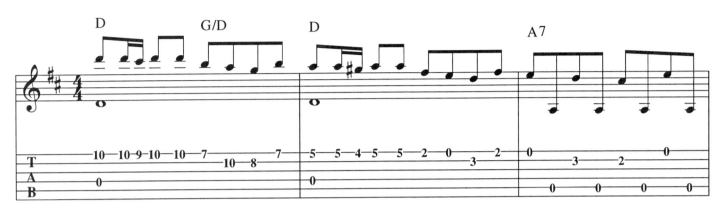

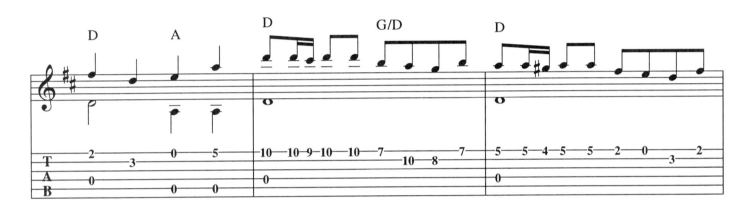

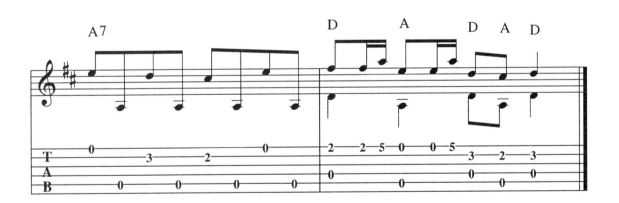

Chords for strumming

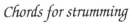

ad lib (let high E ring)

Waltz of the Flowers

from "The Nutcracker"

P. I. Tchaikovsky
adapted by Steve Eckels

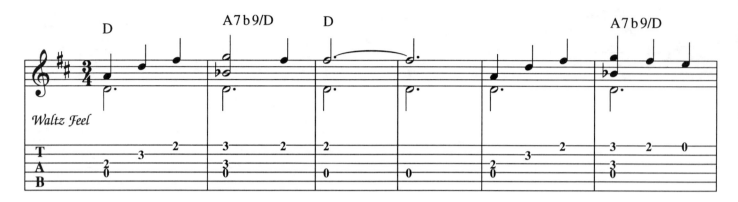

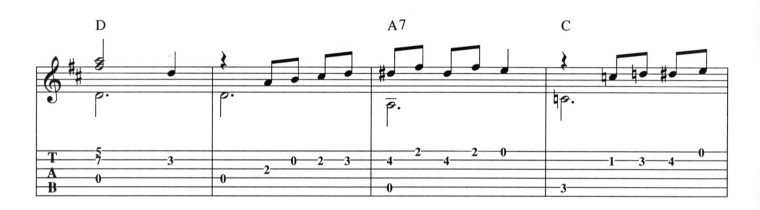

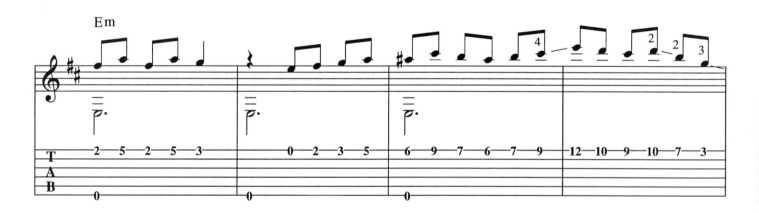

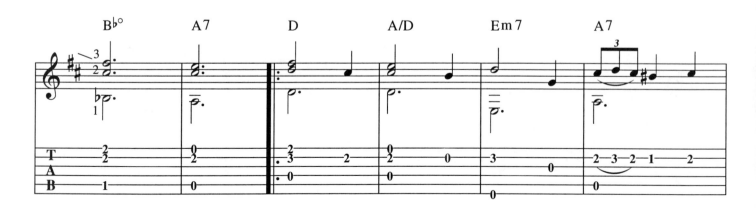

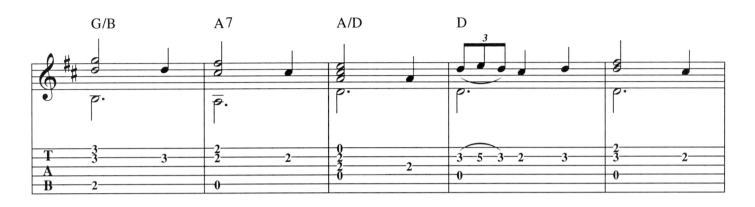

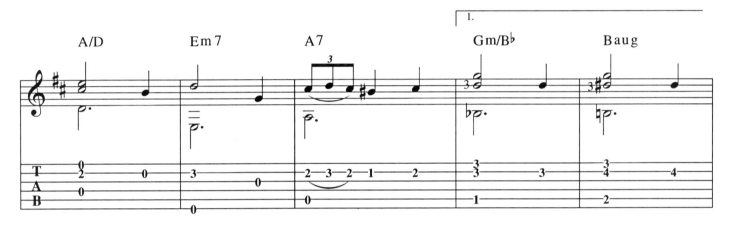

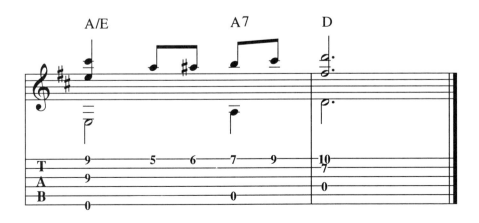

O Come, All Ye Faithful

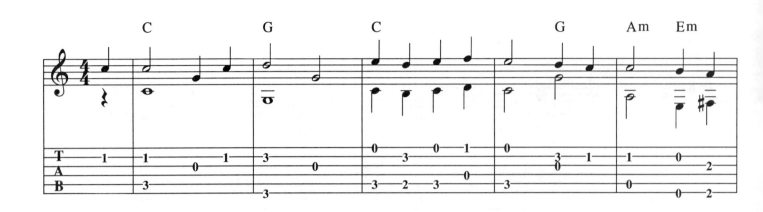

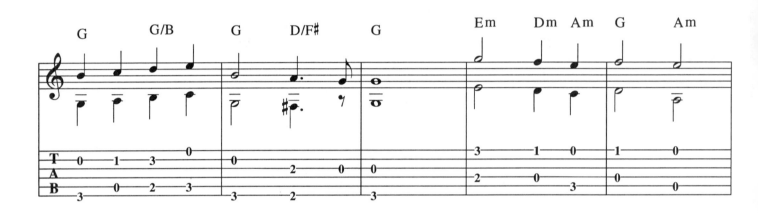

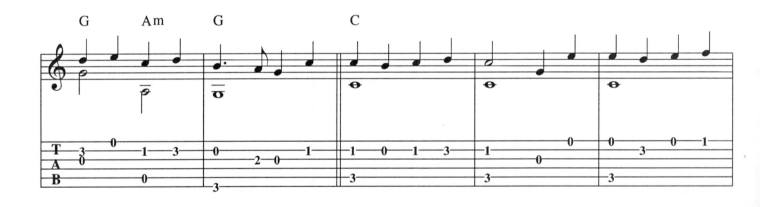

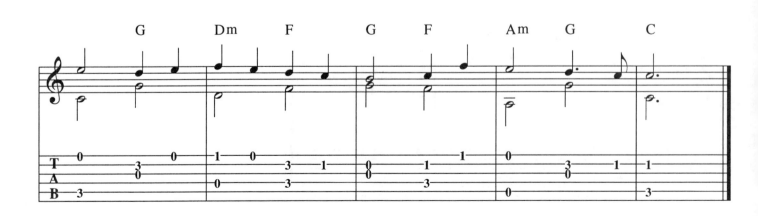

O Come, Little Children

For fun, try this with a
Reggae beat at half tempo.

O Come, Little Children

Key of D

71

O Come, O Come Emmanuel

Key of A minor

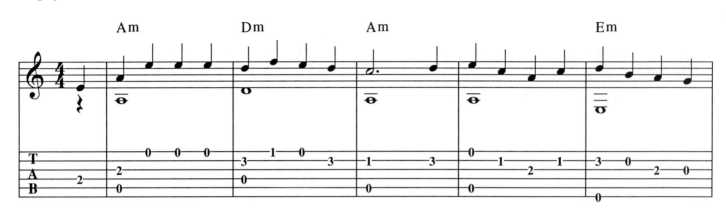

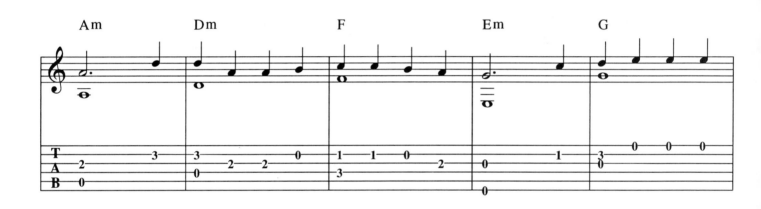

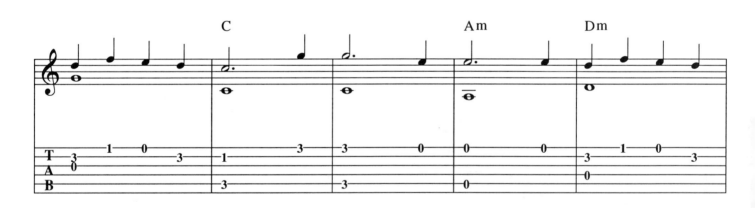

O Come, O Come Emmanuel

Key of E minor

O Holy Night

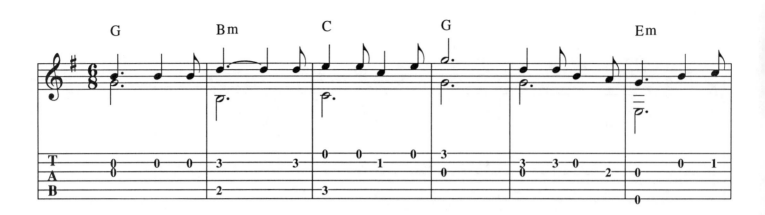

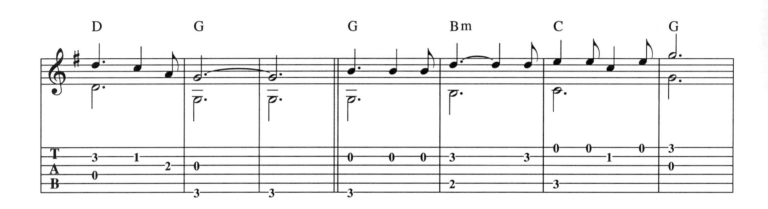

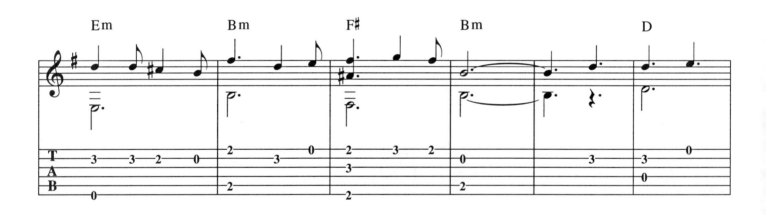

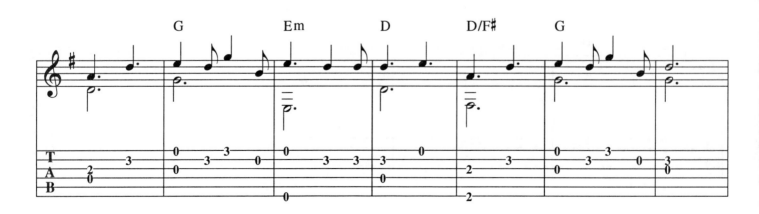

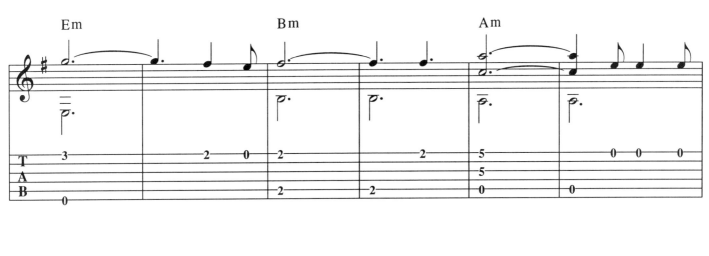

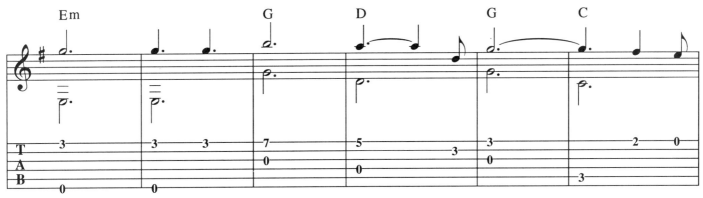

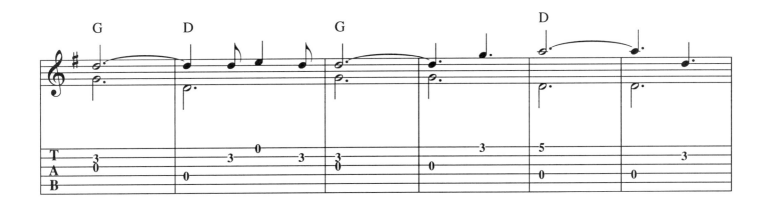

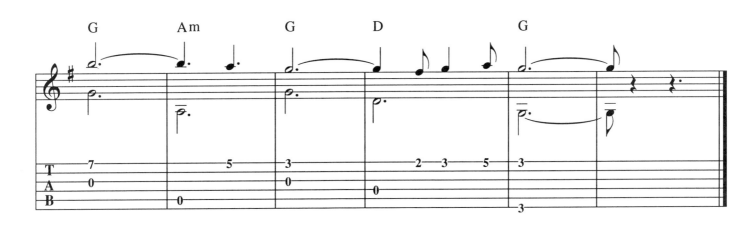

O Sanctissima

Key of G

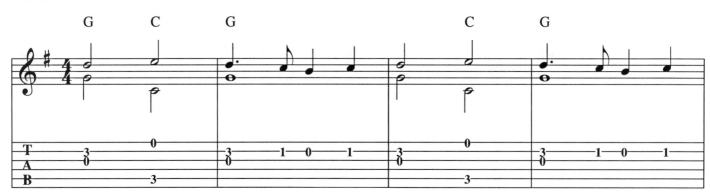

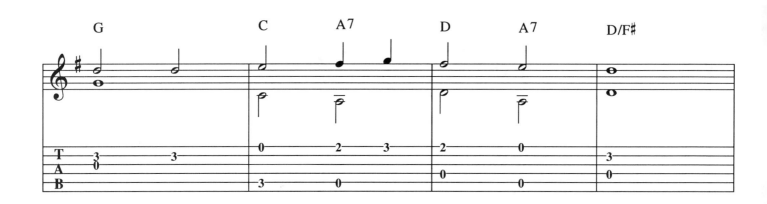

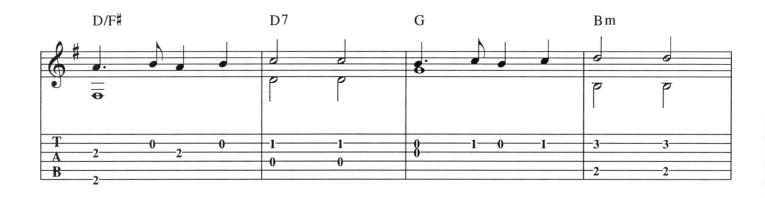

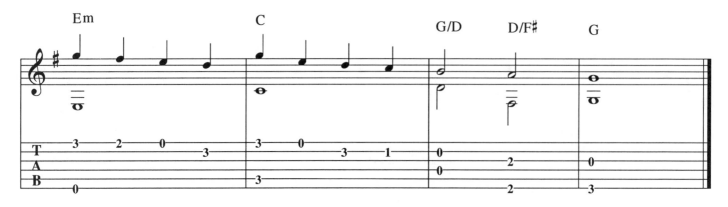

Listen for the theme of the folk song, "We Shall Overcome" in the first four measures.

O Sanctissima

Key of A

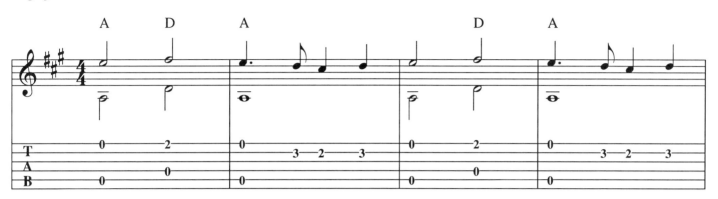

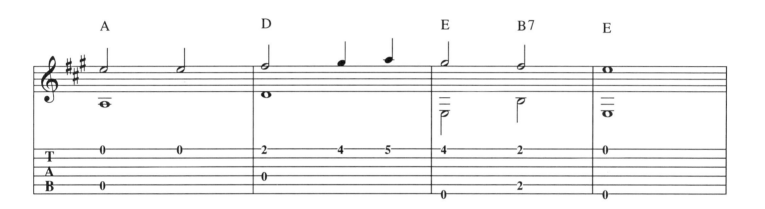

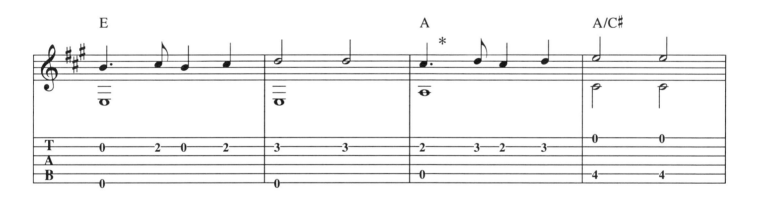

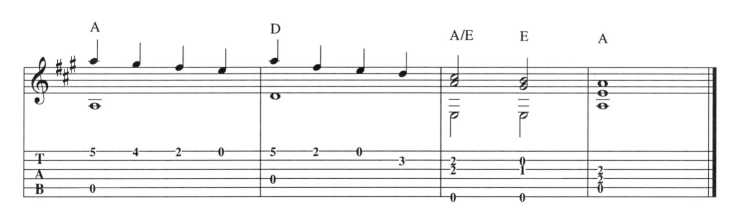

* You may substitute F# minor here.

Of the Father's Love Begotten

In a rhythm like Gregorian Chant

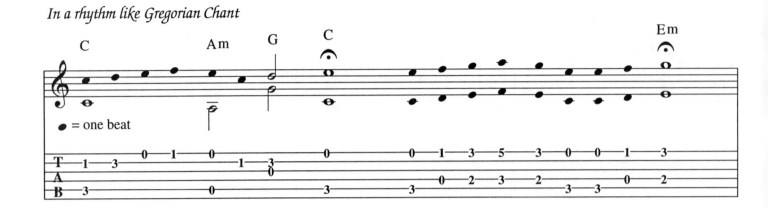

♩ = one beat

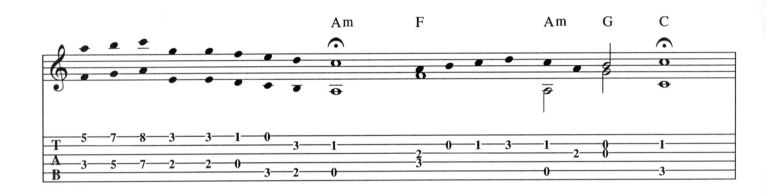

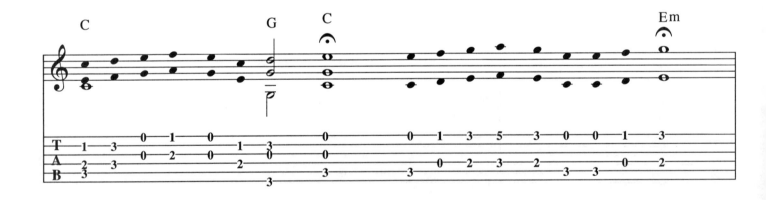

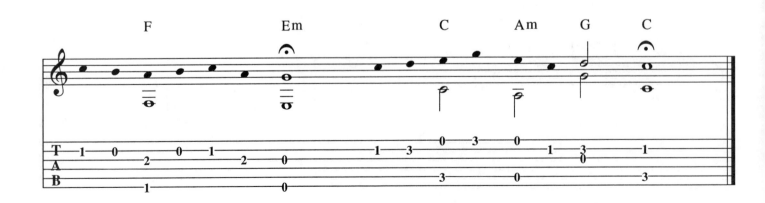

This page has been left blank to avoid awkward page turns.

Oh Christmas Tree

Key of D

Oh Christmas Tree

Key of G

Oh Little Town of Bethlehem

Key of C

Oh Little Town of Bethlehem

Key of D

Pachelbel Canon

adapted by Steve Eckels

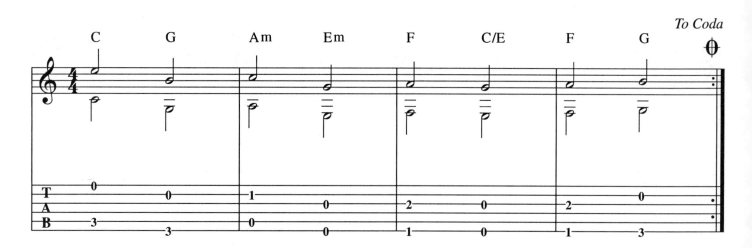

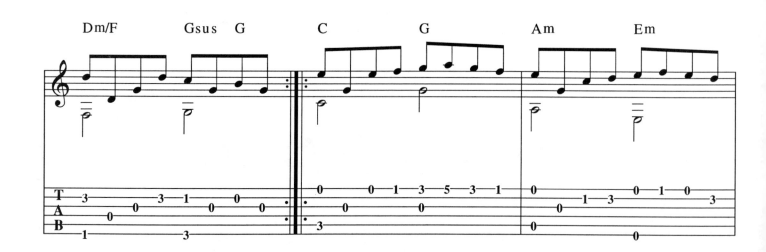

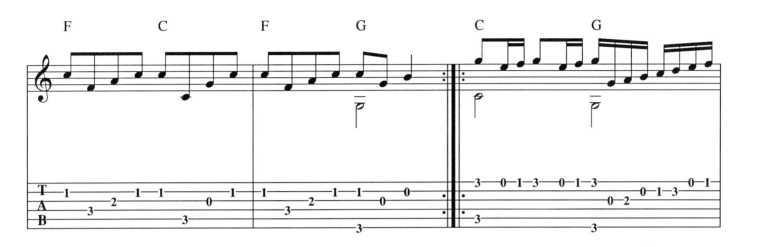

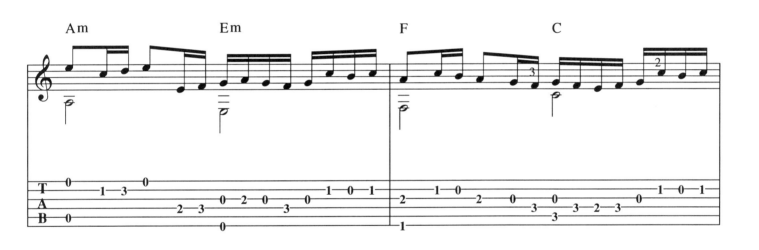

Coda

D.C. al Coda

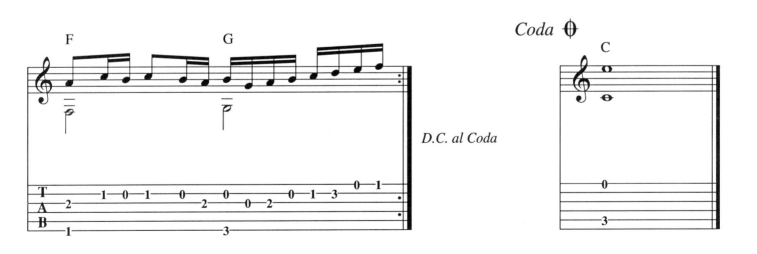

Pat-a-Pan

Key of A minor

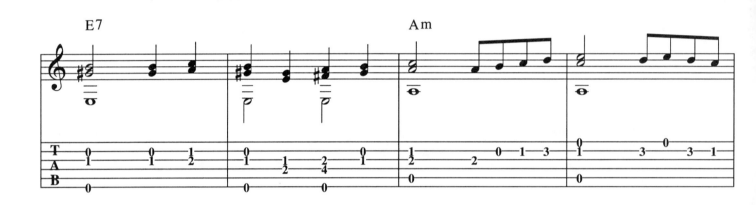

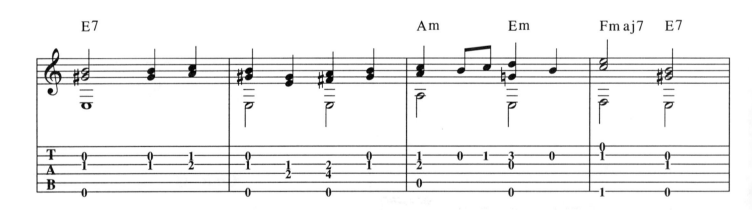

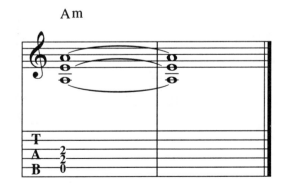

Optional Introduction or Interlude

Pat-a-Pan

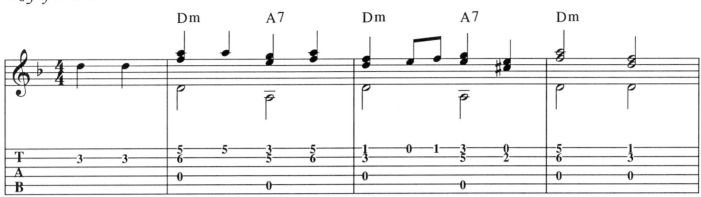

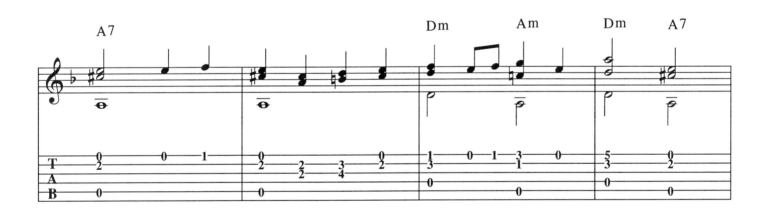

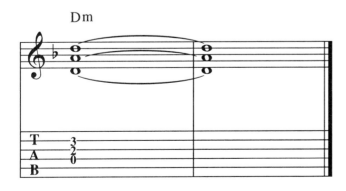

Rise Up Shepherd and Follow

This traditional negro spiritual
makes a nice blues song

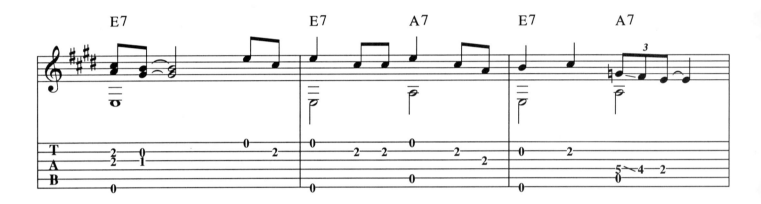

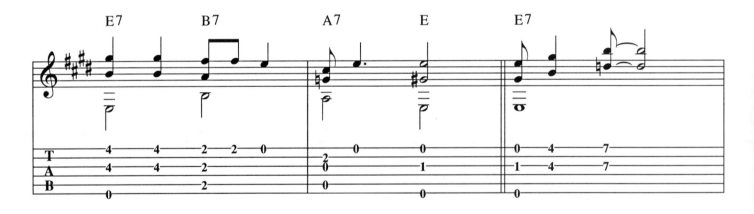

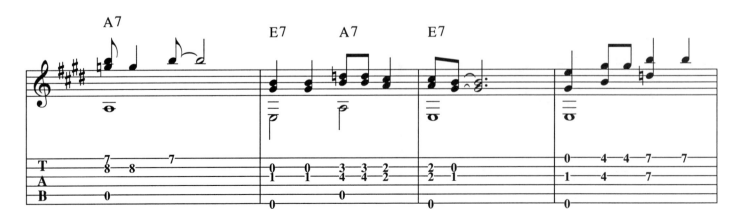

Optional intros and endings

ad lib

Silent Night

Key of G

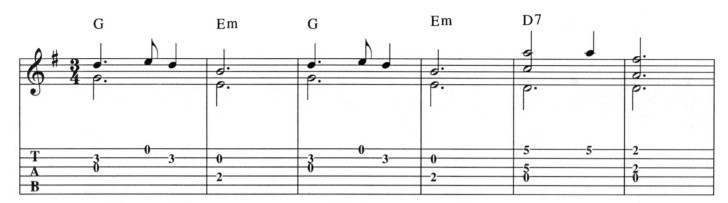

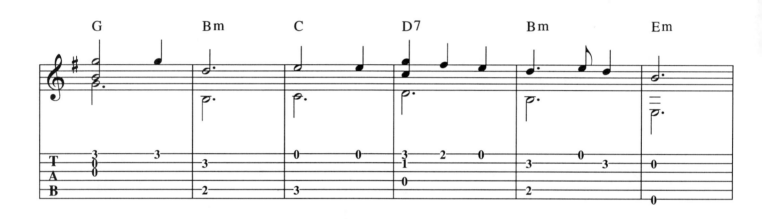

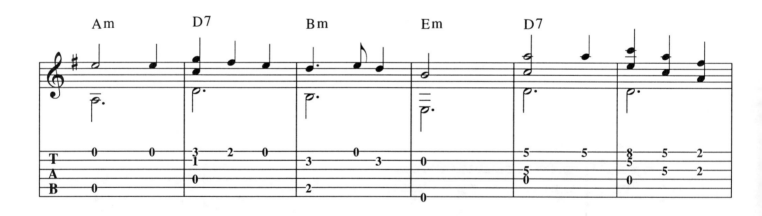

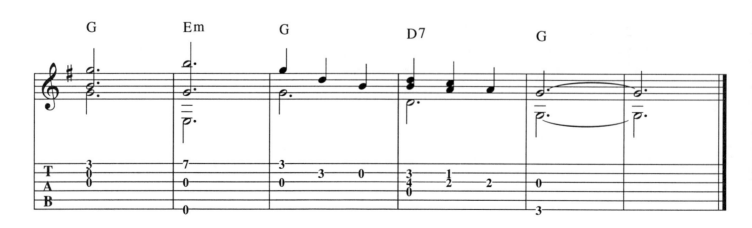

Silent Night

Key of A

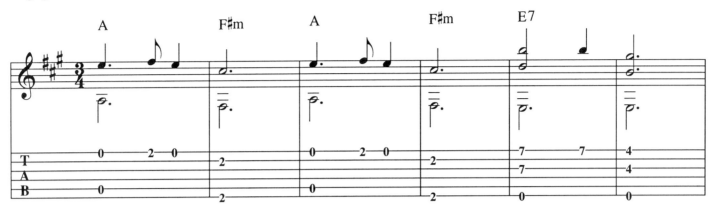

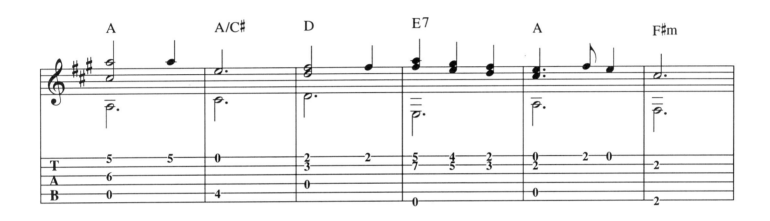

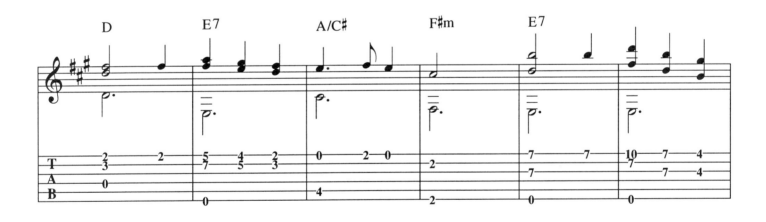

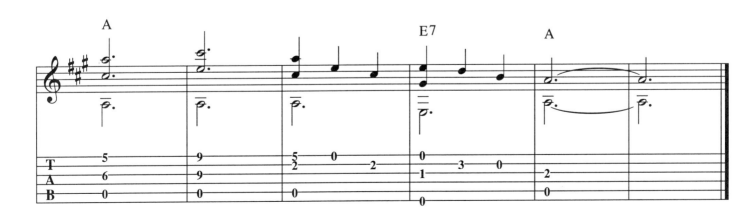

The Snow Lay on the Ground

Key of D

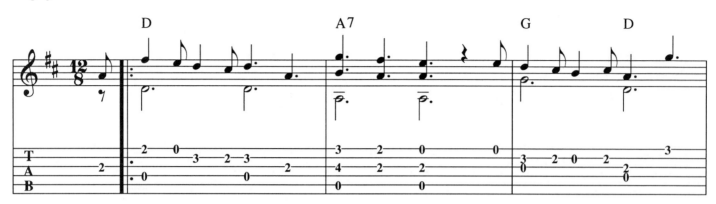

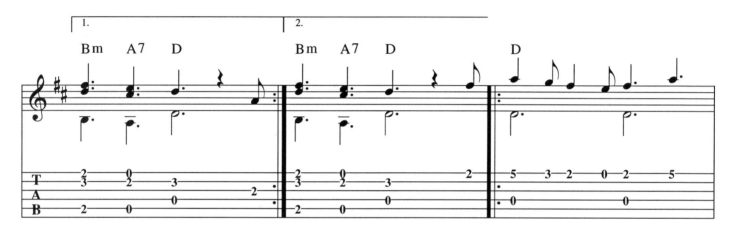

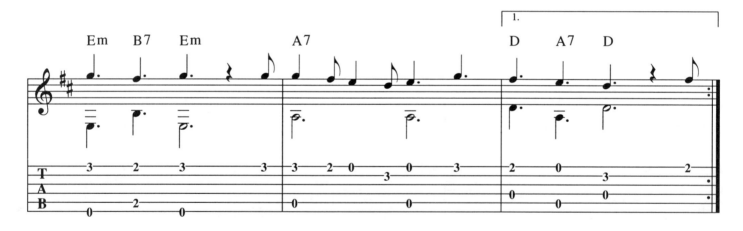

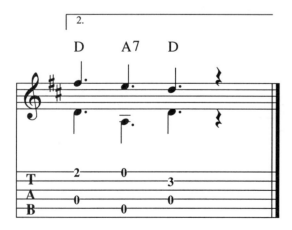

The Snow Lay on the Ground

Key of A

'Twas in the Moon of Wintertime

Easy version

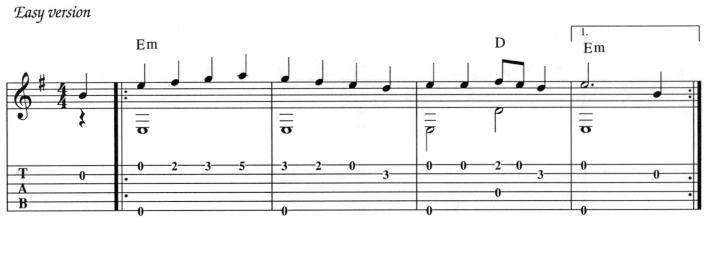

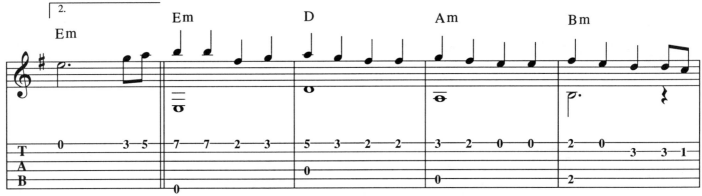

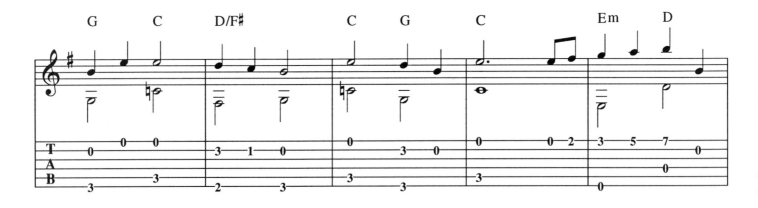

Optional Introduction and Interlude

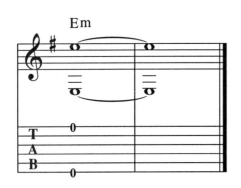

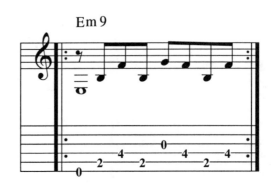

'Twas in the Moon of Wintertime

Intermediate Level

The Twelve Days of Christmas

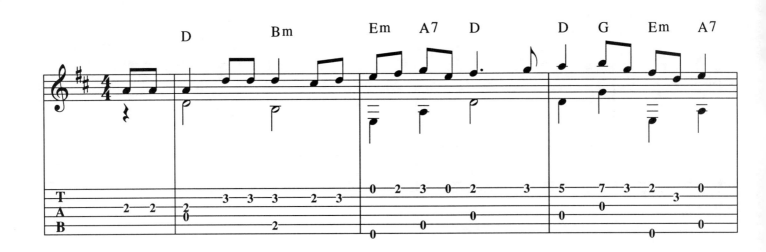

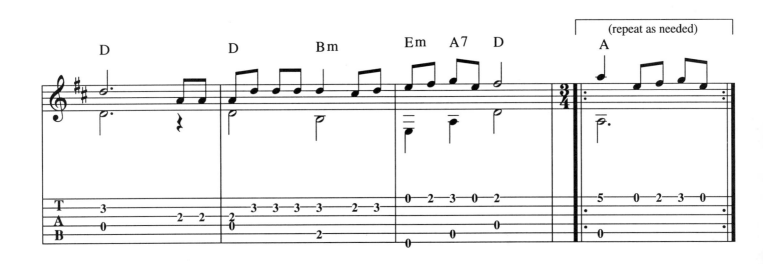

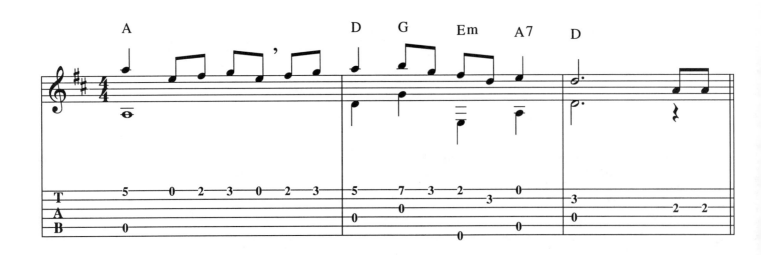

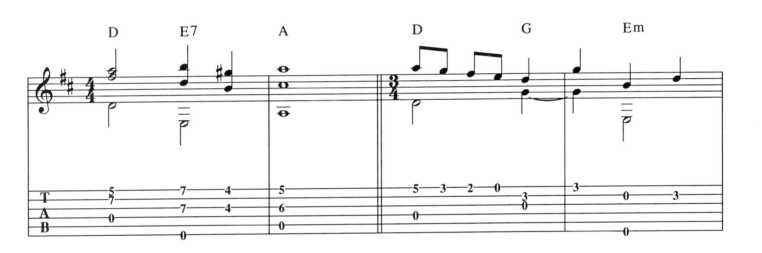

Watchman, Tell Us of the Night

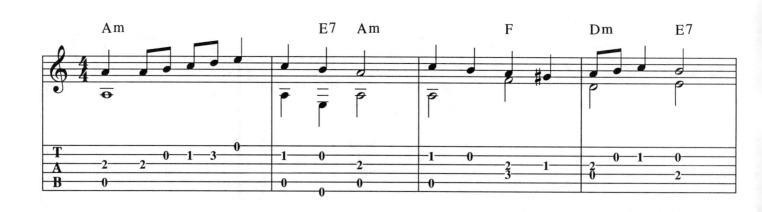

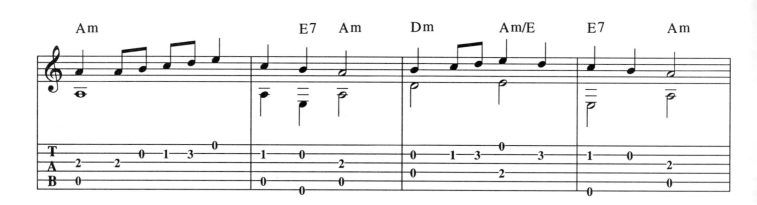

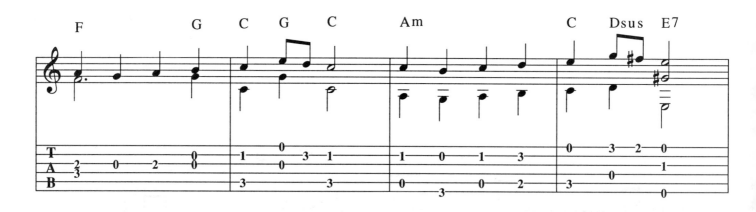

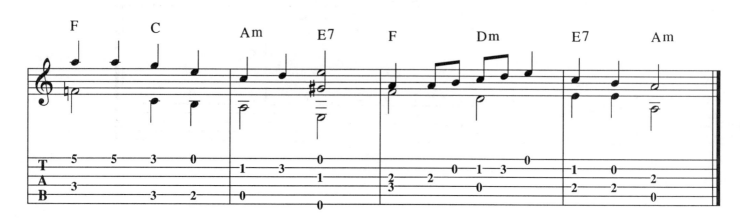

We Three Kings

We Wish You a Merry Christmas

Key of D

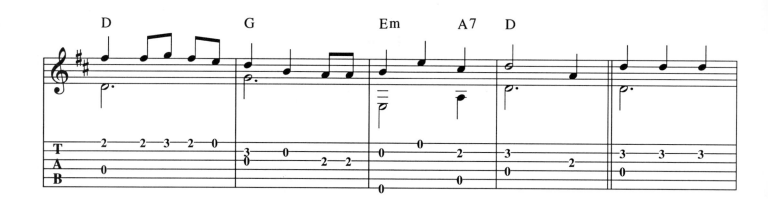

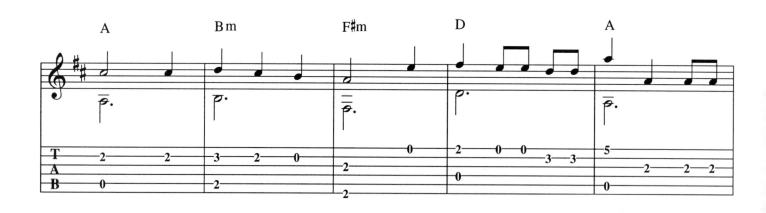

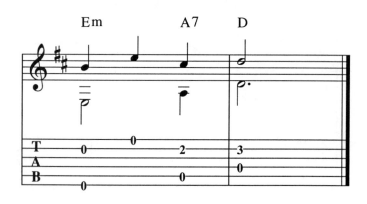

We Wish You a Merry Christmas

Key of G

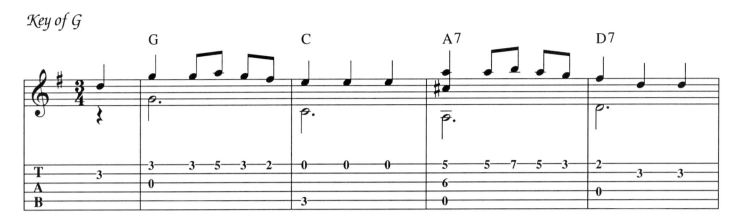

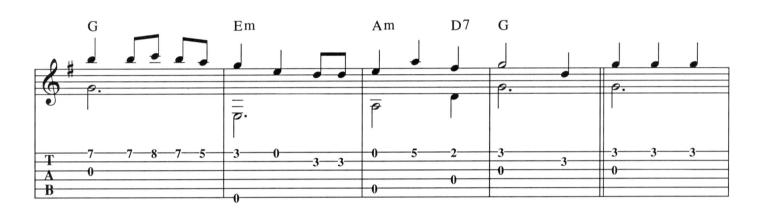

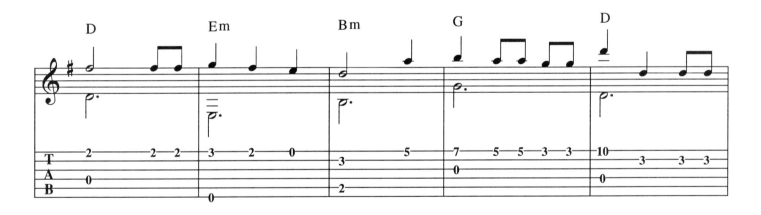

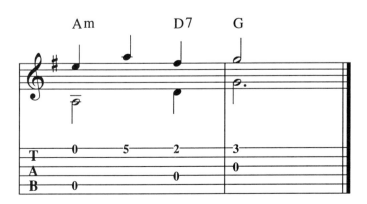

What Child is This?

Key of A minor

What Child is This?

Key of E minor

Burning Candles on the Street

(Nerot Dolkim)

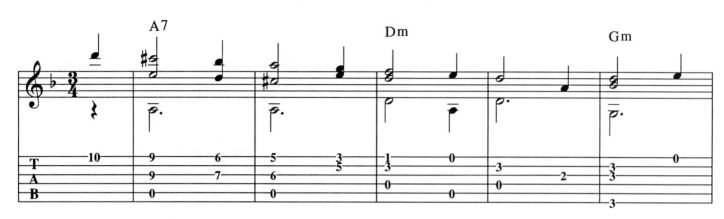

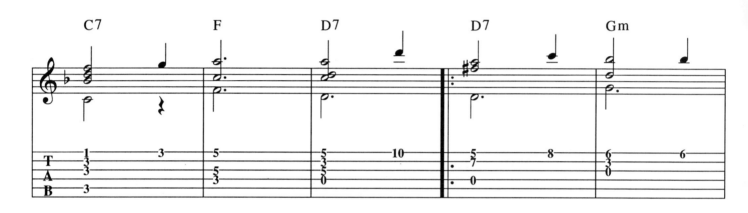

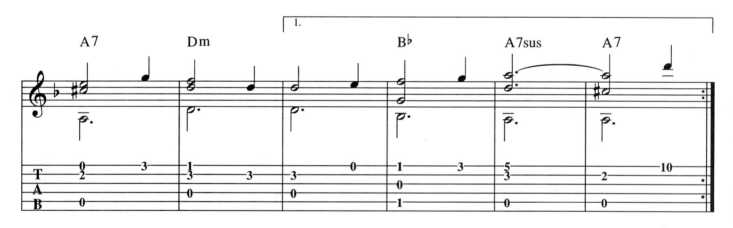

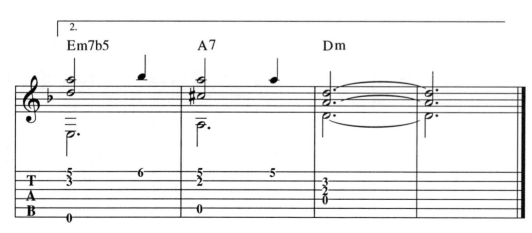

Dreydl Turn

(S' Vivon)

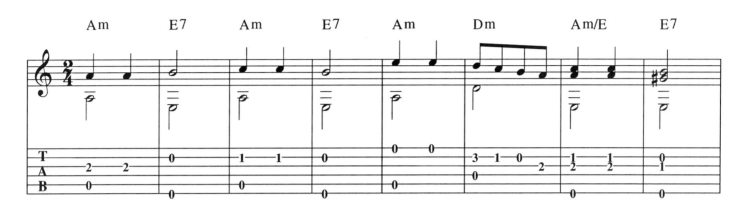

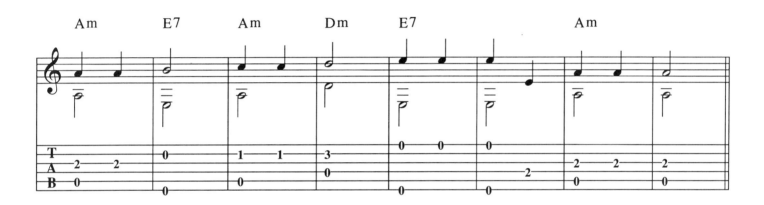

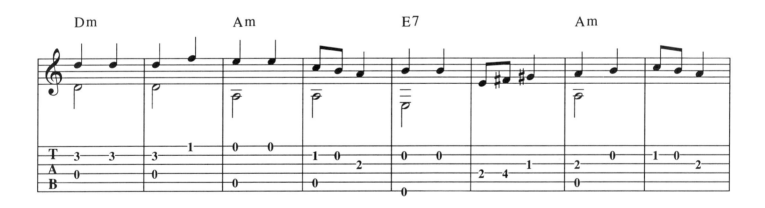

I Have a Little Dreydl
(Ich Hawb ah Klaynem Dreydl)

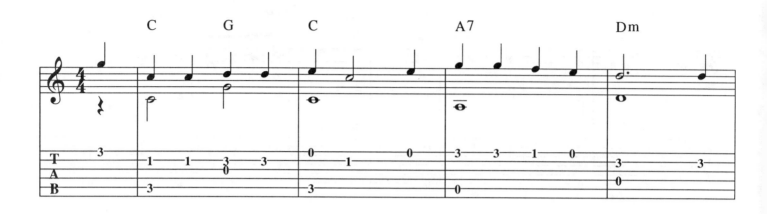

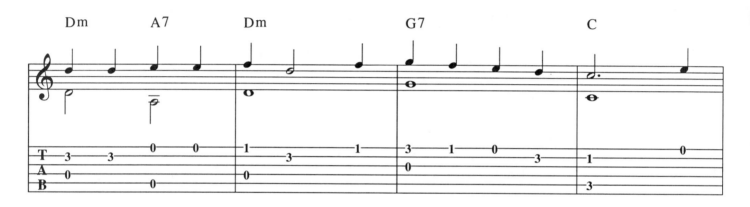

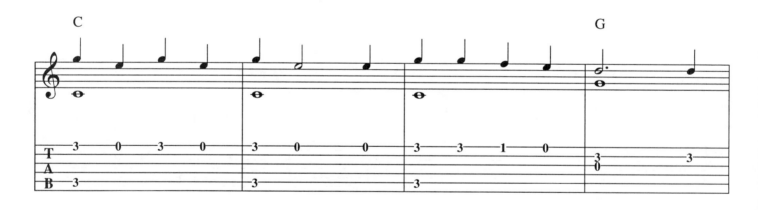

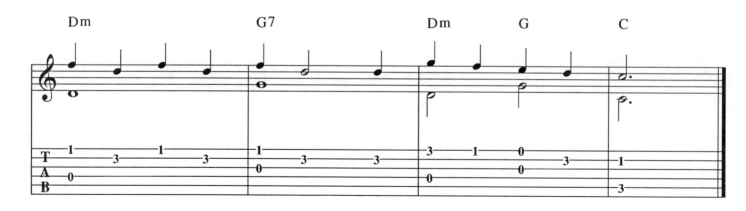

My Little Candle

(Ner Li)

O You Little Candle Lights
(O Ir Kleine Lichtelech)

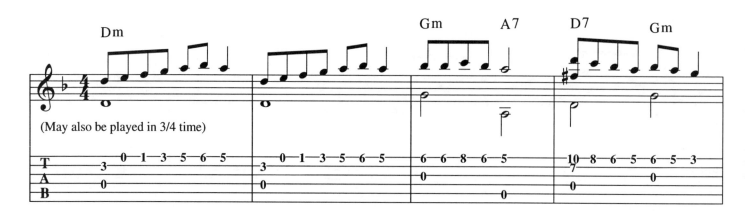

(May also be played in 3/4 time)

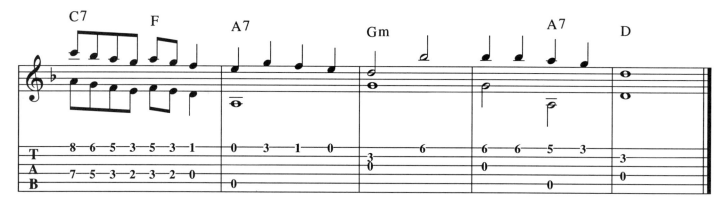

Rock of Ages
(Maoz Tzur)

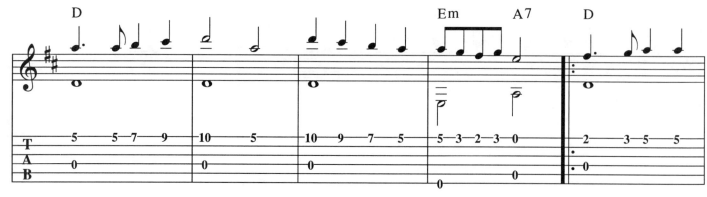

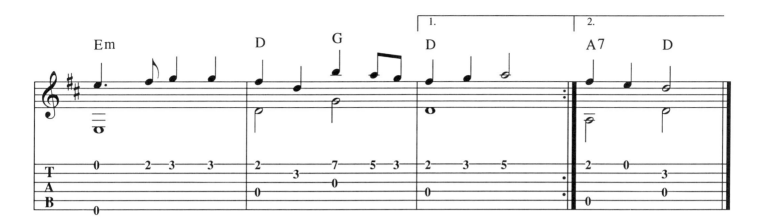

These Candles

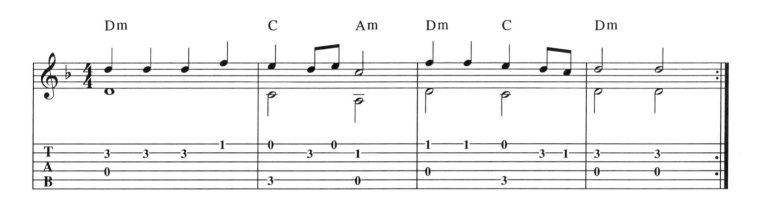

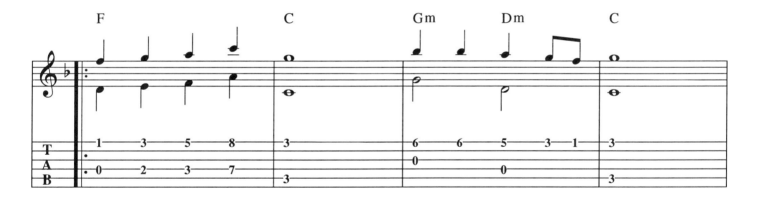

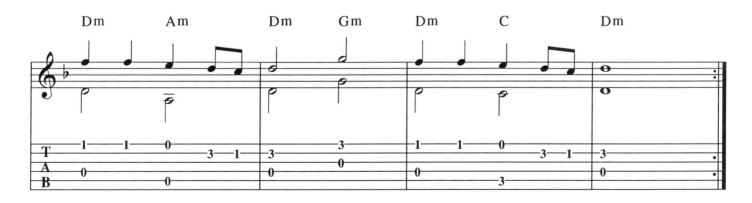

These Candles We Light

(Hanerot Halalu)

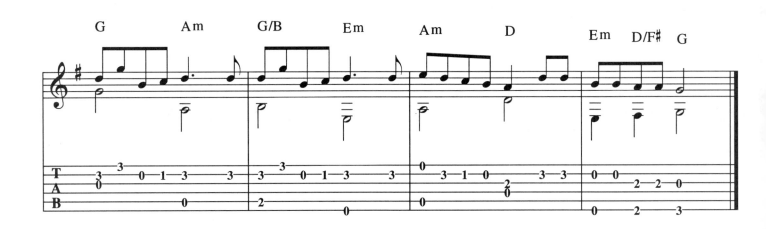

Who Can Retell?

(Mi Yemaleil?)

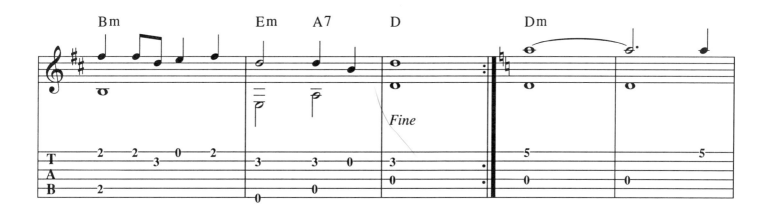

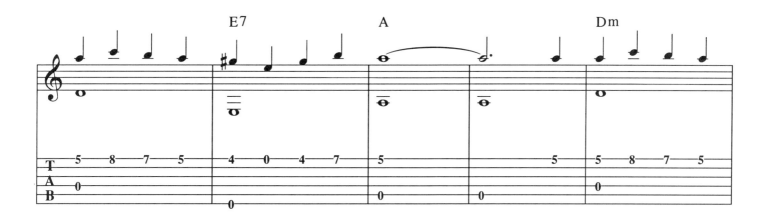

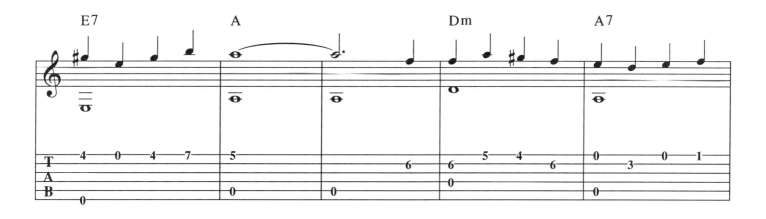

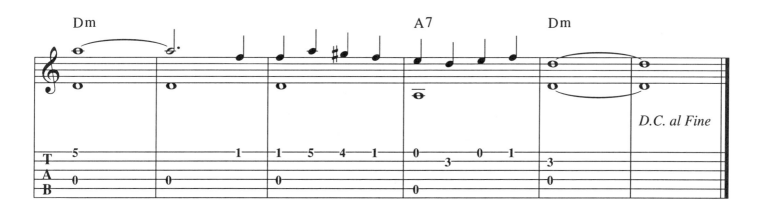

Who Lit the Tiny Candles?

(Mi Ze Hidlik)

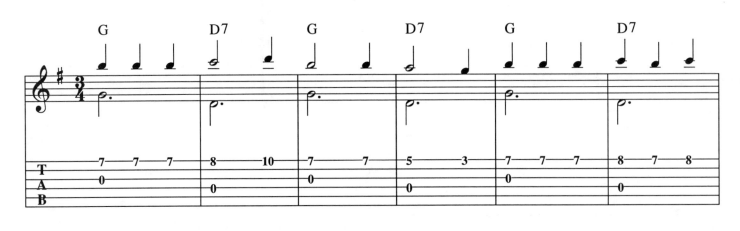

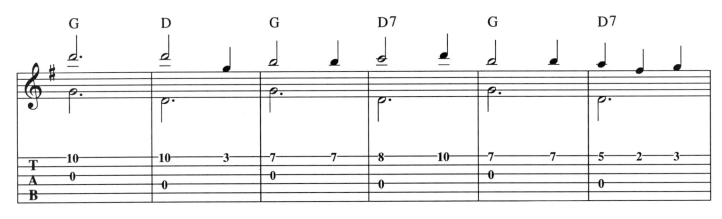

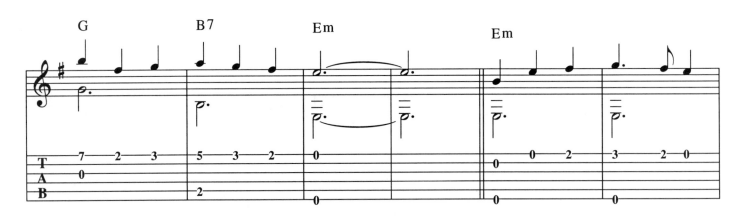

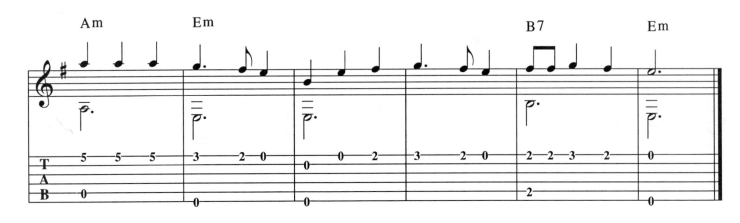

Steve Eckels

Steve Eckels has a Master's degree in guitar from New England Conservatory, a Bachelor's degree in guitar from Berklee College of Music, and Music Education Certification from Northland College in Ashland, Wisconsin. He has written several book/CD sets for Mel Bay Publications, including *Blues Classics for Acoustic Guitar* (95273BCD), *Cowboy Songs for Acoustic Guitar* (97250BCD), *Fingerstyle Blues Method* (98293BCD), *Gospel Classics for Acoustic Guitar* (95704BCD), *Gregorian Chants for Acoustic Guitar* (96651BCD), and *Music of the North American Indians for Acoustic Guitar* (96015BCD). He has six self-produced compact discs currently available through his own mail order catalog at guitarmusicman.com. He has taught guitar privately to children and adults as well as at the college level.

Alphabetical Listing of Contents

Author's Note

The arrangements in this book have been designed for use by the beginner and professional alike. The arrangements consist primarily of the melody, bass and chord symbols so that the professional will be able to easily sight read and embellish them during holiday performances. The beginner will find them straightforward and will be able to learn them quickly. To add variety, I have presented many of the songs in two keys or versions and the pages are laid out to avoid awkward page turns during performance. It was my intent to include all of the well known Christmas favorites plus some lesser known gems. In addition to Christmas carols, many of the greatest melodies associated with Christmas have been included. Some of these are: Selections from the *Nutcracker*; Jesu, Joy of Man's Desiring; Ave Maria; the Pastorale from the *Christmas Concerto* by Corelli; Pachelbel's Canon and others. As a bonus, I have included ten popular Chanukah songs for Jewish celebrations.

It is my sincere hope that this book provides you with years of pleasure and use. I have recorded embellished versions of many of these songs on my Christmas recordings "In the Moon of Wintertime" and "Comfort and Joy", which are available through my website, www.guitarmusicman.com.

Peace,

Steve Eckels

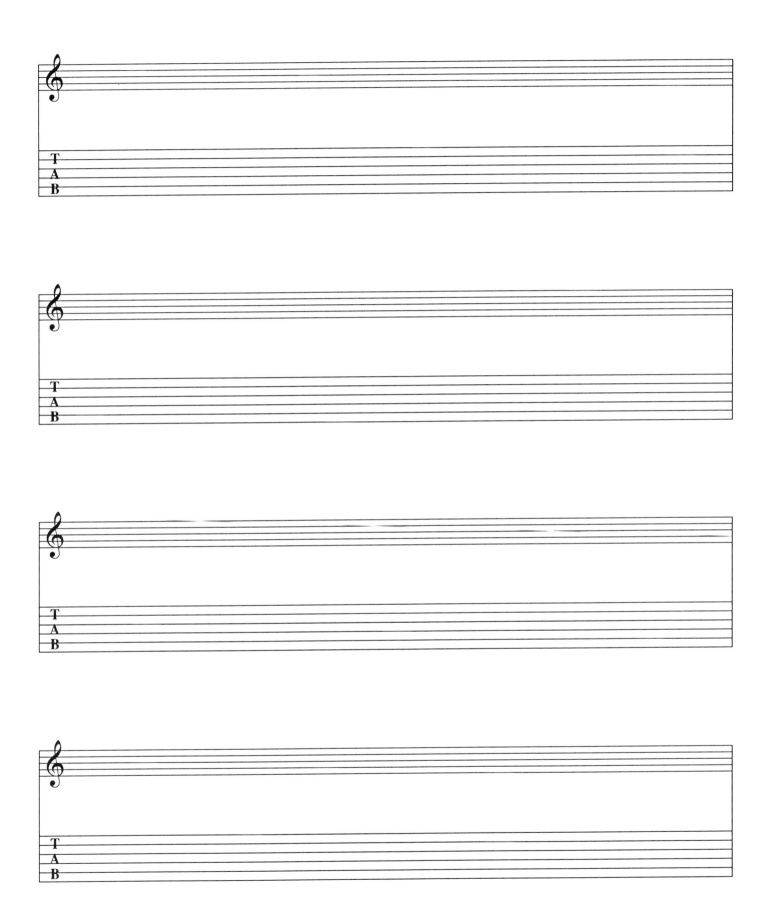

EXCELLENCE IN MUSIC

MEL BAY®

Since 1947